ARKANA

ON HAVING NO HEAD

D. E. Harding is no blinkered specialist. While a partner in a flourishing architectural practice, he taught comparative religion for Cambridge University. While a wartime major, he developed a unique means to spiritual enlightenment. He describes his field as the meeting-place of psychology, physical science, philosophy and religion. His published works include *Head Off Stress* (Arkana 1990), a whodunnit, a philosophical treatise that took eight years to write, books on religion and the arts of living and dying and articles in the *Transactional Analysis Journal*, *Architectural Review*, *Middle Way* and the *Saturday Evening Post*. Ann Bancroft's *20th Century Mystics and Sages* has a chapter on Harding as 'the man without a head' – a reputation which the Incredible String Band helped to establish with their *Douglas Harding Song*. At the age of eighty he still conducts workshops around the world. Attendances – and 'decapitations' – have ranged from a handful to thousands.

D. E. HARDING

ON HAVING NO HEAD

ZEN AND THE REDISCOVERY
OF THE OBVIOUS

FOREWORD BY HUSTON SMITH

ARKANA

To Virginia Parsell, Barbara Hopkinson
and Gene Thursby

ARKANA

Published by the Penguin Group
Penguin Books Ltd, 27 Wrights Lane, London W8 5TZ, England
Viking Penguin, a division of Penguin Books USA Inc.
375 Hudson Street, New York, New York 10014, USA
Penguin Books Australia Ltd, Ringwood, Victoria, Australia
Penguin Books Canada Ltd, 2801 John Street, Markham, Ontario, Canada L3R 1B4
Penguin Books (NZ) Ltd, 182–190 Wairau Road, Auckland 10, New Zealand

Penguin Books Ltd, Registered Offices: Harmondsworth, Middlesex, England

This edition first published by Arkana 1986
5 7 9 10 8 6

Printed in England by Clays Ltd, St Ives plc

Contents

FOREWORD by Huston Smith vi

PREFACE by Gene R. Thursby.................................... ix

1 THE TRUE SEEING... 1
2 MAKING SENSE OF THE SEEING 5
3 DISCOVERING ZEN 21
4 BRINGING THE STORY UP TO DATE 35
  The Eight Stages of the Headless Way:
  (1) The Headless Infant 36
  (2) The Child 37
  (3) The Headed Grown-up................................ 38
  (4) The Headless Seer...................................... 42
  (5) Practising Headlessness............................. 50
  (6) Working It Out 56
  (7) The Barrier.. 70
  (8) The Breakthrough....................................... 73
     Summary and Conclusion.............................. 76

POSTSCRIPT.. 78

Foreword

The best way for me to introduce the reader to the revised edition of this book is to relate how its original edition first fell into my hands.

It was 1961 and, returning from university lectures in Australia, I had scheduled a stop in Bangkok to discuss with John Blofeld his recently published translations of *The Zen Teachings of Huang Po* and *The Zen Teachings of Hui Hai*. We had scarcely settled into our conversations when in reference to some point I had raised he reached for a slim volume on his rattan coffee table which he said had arrived out of the blue the week before; it was this book in hand. I do not recall the point he used it to amplify, but I remember vividly his enthusiasm for the book itself. "I have no idea who this man Harding is," he said: "he may be a London cabbie for all I know. But he's got it just right."

The next day as I was saying my farewells Blofeld again reached for the book, this time insisting that I take it with me for flight reading. By then my curiosity was such that I did not even go through the motions of protesting his generosity, so high over the Pacific I had the opportunity to check out his assessment. It was accurate. Harding had indeed gotten it just right.

Foreword

Not that the magic will work for everyone; one can never be sure that words will produce the effects they intend. But I know of no other piece of writing as concise as the opening chapter of this book that stands a better chance of shifting the reader's perception to a different register. And the reason is clear. Insight derives from images more than it does from reasoning, and the image Harding hit on is a powerful one. "I have no head." Outrageous on first hearing, the author stays with the claim - circling it, returning to it, until (as with *ko-ans* that likewise sound absurd on first hearing) a barrier breaks and we see, not something different, but in a different way.

Light breaks on secret lots.
When logics die,
Truth jumps through the eye.

Perhaps it is because I first read this book on a plane that my mind goes back to another airborne moment when I was seated beside a tiny whitehaired lady who, though she was in her eighties, was experiencing her first flight. She was not talkative, but at one point, 32,000 feet above Grand Rapids, she turned to me and asked matter-of-factly, in perfect calm, "Why have we stopped?" I started in my seat - then almost immediately, smiling at her naïvety, I relaxed. But not quite into my previous prosaic state. Hurtling through space without a trace of sound or motion was no longer commonplace. The world was green again with wonder, and mined almost carelessly with surprise.

If, as Castenada's Yaqui shaman, Don Juan, teaches, we must "stop the world" in its routine spinning if we are to truly see, my companion's startling question over Michigan, and Harding's startling claim over the Pacific - "I have no head" - caused me to do just that.

This revised edition brings several improvements. The scope of the book has been widened to include parallels in traditions other than Buddhism, and a concluding chapter on "the head-less way" has been added to relate the book's central insight to the daily round. But the insight itself remains central, as it should. *Anatta*, no self (read: no permanent, individual self) is not only the key to Buddhism; rightly understood, it is the key to life. "The less of self there is," Eckhart wrote, "the more there is of Self."

Intuitively we see this; we know that we see better when we stop standing in our own light. But it is one of those things that we know but never learn, so we need to be reminded of it repeatedly. Or better, we need to have it break over us in fresh ways, which is the prospect this book extends.

We might think of Harding as approaching us as a *roshi* in disguise, a teacher garbed, of all things, in book covers. If we are to be worthy students we must be prepared for instruction from any quarter.

Huston Smith
Hanna Professor of Philosophy
Hamline University
Saint Paul, Minnesota

Preface

Long before the fictitious Hitchhiker's Guide to the Galaxy *became famous in these regions, this similarly small, cheap, and wide-ranging book was circulating throughout the world—making its way from friend to friend. Copies have been seen not only on coffee tables but on mountain trails, in hostels, homes, and schools. Those copies tend to be well-worn, a bit curled at the edges, but centrally sound just like those who continue to take delight in them. For the message of this book seems to go deep, to touch the heart, and to encourage people to acknowledge and share their inmost awareness.*

It is not (thank goodness) an academic book, nor should it make difficult reading. In any event its method and meaning are complemented by some fine recent studies. Jacob Needleman's account of the transformation of our lives by ideas (in contrast to concepts) in The Heart of Philosophy, *Ken Wilber's discussion of the simplicity of ultimate consciousness (and the ways of resisting it) in* No Boundary: Eastern and Western Approaches to Personal Growth, *Dr. Arthur Deikman's distinction between observing and object self in* The Observing Self: Mysticism and Psychotherapy, *and specially Huston Smith's work on the reorienting power of key perceptions (vs. routine ones) in his* Beyond the Post-Modern Mind, *are contemporary examples of the analysis of what Douglas Harding presents to us first-hand and first-person in a simple but most penetrating way.*

Preface

Since its initial publication in 1961, On Having No Head *has become something of a modern classic of the life of the spirit. In addition to British and North American editions, a short selection was included in Hofstadter and Dennett's anthology,* The Mind's I: Fantasies and Reflections on Self and Soul *(1981), but the excerpt which appeared there tends to obscure the full meaning of Harding's message and makes the appearance of this new edition all the more welcome. On the Continent a French translation by Jean Van Harck was published in Paris in 1978 under the title* Vivre sans tête, *and a German translation of the current edition is expected to be completed and published in 1985.*

Among Mr. Harding's other achievements have been a career in architecture; a large number of written works on the same theme as the present one – some of them not yet published – the most distinguished and difficult among them The Hierarchy of Heaven and Earth: A New Diagram of Man in the Universe, *with an enthusiastic preface by the Christian scholar C.S. Lewis; a patented three-dimensional model called the* Youniverse Explorer; *and an on-going series of international workshops to share the central insight of this book.*

But this book is not about Douglas Harding. Nor is it about anything narrowly intellectual, organizational, or religious. It is about and for the one who is reading this, right now.

Gene R. Thursby
Associate Professor of Religion
University of Florida
Gainesville, Florida

The author has asked me to emphasize the following:

Having already got to the very heart of this book in the first few pages (where it is wholly obvious and wholly available) the reader should not be surprised or thrown if he or she goes on to find some of what follows anything but obvious, and as yet of little use. To see into one's true Nature (or headlessness) is to be one's own authority, to adventure down a unique Path and to make one's own discoveries. The author's purpose - while providing illustrations drawn from his own experience - is to encourage true Self-reliance. As Emerson wrote: "A man should learn to detect and watch that gleam of light which flashes across his mind from within, more than the lustre of the firmament of bards and sages."

Suppose a man were all of a sudden to make his appearance here and cut your head off with a sword!

HUI-CHUNG

Behead yourself!... Dissolve your whole body into Vision: become seeing, seeing, seeing!

RUMI

My soul has been carried away, and usually my head as well, without my being able to prevent it.

ST. TERESA

Cover your breast with nothingness, and draw over your head the robe of non-existence.

ATTAR

Give yourself utterly... Even though the head itself must be given, why should you weep over it?

KABIR

Seeing into Nothingness – this is the true seeing, the eternal seeing.

SHEN-HUI

1
The True Seeing

The best day of my life – my rebirthday, so to speak – was when I found I had no head. This is not a literary gambit, a witticism designed to arouse interest at any cost. I mean it in all seriousness: I have no head.

It was when I was thirty-three that I made the discovery. Though it certainly came out of the blue, it did so in response to an urgent inquiry; I had for several months been absorbed in the question: *what am I?* The fact that I happened to be walking in the Himalayas at the time probably had little to do with it; though in that country unusual states of mind are said to come more easily. However that may be, a very still clear day, and a view from the ridge where I stood, over misty blue valleys to the highest mountain range in the world, made a setting worthy of the grandest vision.

What actually happened was something absurdly simple and unspectacular: just for the moment I stopped thinking. Reason and imagination and all mental chatter died down. For once, words really failed me. I forgot my name, my humanness, my thingness, all that could be called me or mine. Past and future dropped away. It was as if I had been born that instant, brand new, mindless, innocent of all memories. There existed only the Now, that present moment and what was clearly given in it. To

1

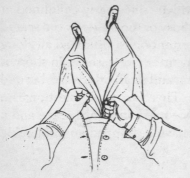

look was enough. And what I found was khaki trouserlegs terminating downwards in a pair of brown shoes, khaki sleeves terminating sideways in a pair of pink hands, and a khaki shirtfront terminating upwards in – absolutely nothing whatever! Certainly not in a head.

It took me no time at all to notice that this nothing, this hole where a head should have been, was no ordinary vacancy, no mere nothing. On the contrary, it was very much occupied. It was a vast emptiness vastly filled, a nothing that found room for everything - room for grass, trees, shadowy distant hills, and far above them snow-peaks like a row of angular clouds riding the blue sky. I had lost a head and gained a world.

It was all, quite literally, breathtaking. I seemed to stop breathing altogether, absorbed in the Given. Here it was, this superb scene, brightly shining in the clear air, alone and unsupported, mysteriously suspended in the void, and (and this was the real miracle, the wonder and delight) utterly free of "me", unstained by any observer. Its total presence was my total absence, body and soul. Lighter than air, clearer than glass, altogether released from myself, I was nowhere around.

Yet in spite of the magical and uncanny quality of this vision, it was no dream, no esoteric revelation. Quite the reverse: it felt like a sudden waking from the sleep of ordinary life, an end to dreaming. It was self-luminous reality for once swept clean of all obscuring mind. *It was the revelation, at long last, of the perfectly obvious.* It was a lucid moment in a confused life-history. It was a

2

ceasing to ignore something which (since early childhood at any rate) I had always been too busy or too clever or too scared to see. It was naked, uncritical attention to what had all along been staring me in the face - my utter facelessness. In short, it was all perfectly simple and plain and straightforward, beyond argument, thought, and words. There arose no questions, no reference beyond the experience itself, but only peace and a quiet joy, and the sensation of having dropped an intolerable burden.

*The notion that man has a body distinct from his soul is to be expunged;
this I shall do by... melting apparent surfaces away, and displaying the
infinite which was hid.*

BLAKE

*"I think I'll go and meet her," said Alice... "You can't possibly do that,"
said the Rose: "I should advise you to walk the other way."
This sounded nonsense to Alice, so she said nothing, but set off at once
towards the Red Queen. To her surprise, she lost sight of her in a
moment.*

THROUGH THE LOOKING GLASS

*As a beauty I am not a star;
There are others more handsome by far,
But my face - I don't mind it
For I am behind it;
It's the people in front get the jar.*

Attributed to WOODROW WILSON

2
Making sense of the Seeing

As the first wonder of my Himalayan discovery began to wear off, I started describing it to myself in some such words as the following.

Somehow or other I had vaguely thought of myself as inhabiting this house which is my body, and looking out through its two little round windows at the world. Now I find it isn't like that at all. As I gaze into the distance, what is there at this moment to tell me how many eyes I have here - two, or three, or hundreds, or none? In fact, only one window appears on *this* side of my facade, and that one is wide open and frameless and immense, with nobody looking out of it. It is always the other fellow who has eyes and a face to frame them; never this one.

There exist, then, two sorts - two widely different species - of human being. The first, of which I note countless specimens, evidently carries a head on its shoulders (and by "head" I mean an opaque and coloured and hairy eight-inch ball with various holes in it) while the second, of which I note only one specimen, evidently carries no such thing on its shoulders. And until now I had overlooked this considerable difference! Victim of a prolonged fit of madness, of a lifelong hallucination (and by "hallucination" I mean what my dictionary says: apparent perception of an object not actually present), I had invariably seen myself as

5

pretty much like other people, and certainly never as a decapitated but still living biped. I had been blind to the one thing that is always present, and without which I am blind indeed – to this marvellous substitute-for-a-head, this unbounded clarity, this luminous and absolutely pure void, which nevertheless is – rather than contains – all that's on offer. For, however carefully I attend, I fail to find here even so much as a blank screen on which these mountains and sun and sky are projected, or a clear mirror in which they are reflected, or a transparent lens or aperture through which they are viewed – still less a person to whom they are presented, or a viewer (however shadowy) who is distinguishable from the view. Nothing whatever intervenes, not even that baffling and elusive obstacle called "distance": the visibly boundless blue sky, the pink-edged whiteness of the snows, the sparkling green of the grass – how can these be remote, when there's nothing to be remote from? The headless void here refuses all definition and location: it is not round, or small, or big, or even here as distinct from there. (And even if there *were* a head here to measure outwards from, the measuring-rod stretching from it to that mountain peak would, when read end-on – and there's no other way for me to read it – reduce to a point, to nothing.) In fact, these coloured shapes present themselves in all simplicity, without any such complications as near or far, this or that, mine or not mine, seen-by-me or merely given. All twoness – all duality of subject and object – has vanished: it is no longer read into a situation which has no room for it.

Such were the thoughts which followed the vision. To try to set down the first-hand, immediate experience in these or any other terms, however, is to misrepresent it by complicating what is simplicity itself: indeed the longer the postmortem examination drags on the further it gets from the living original.

At best, these descriptions can remind one of the vision (without the bright awareness) or invite a recurrence of it; but they can no more convey its essential quality, or ensure a recurrence, than the most appetizing menu can taste like the dinner, or the best book about humour enable one to see a joke. On the other hand, it is impossible to stop thinking for long, and some attempt to relate the lucid intervals of one's life to the confused background is inevitable. It could also encourage, indirectly, the recurrence of lucidity.

In any case, there are several common-sense objections which refuse to be put off any longer, questions which insist on reasoned answers, however inconclusive. It becomes necessary to "justify" one's vision, even to oneself; also one's friends may need reassuring. In a sense this attempt at domestication is absurd, because no argument can add to or take from an experience which is as plain and incontrovertible as hearing middle-C or tasting strawberry jam. In another sense, however, the attempt has to be made, if one's life is not to disintegrate into two quite alien, idea-tight compartments.

★　★　★　★　★　★

My first objection was: my head may be missing, but not its nose. Here it is, visibly preceding me wherever I go. And my answer was: if this fuzzy, pinkish, yet perfectly transparent cloud suspended on my right, and this other similar cloud suspended on my left, are noses, then I count two of them and not one; and the perfectly opaque single protuberance which I observe so clearly in the middle of your face is not a nose: only a hopelessly dishonest or confused observer would deliberately use the same name for such utterly different things. I prefer to go by my dictionary and common usage, which oblige me to say that, whereas nearly all human beings have a nose apiece, I have none.

All the same, if some misguided sceptic, over-anxious to make his point, were to strike out in this direction, aiming midway between these two pink clouds, the result would surely be as unpleasant as if I owned the most solid and punchable of noses. Again, what about this complex of subtle tensions, movements, pressures, itches, tickles, aches, warmths, and throbbings, never entirely absent from this central region? Above all, what about these touch-feelings which arise when I explore here with my hand? Surely these findings add up to massive evidence for the existence of my head right here and now after all?

I find they do nothing of the sort. No doubt a great variety of sensations are plainly given here and cannot be ignored, but they don't amount to a head, or anything like one. The only way to make a head out of them would be to throw in all sorts of ingredients that are plainly missing here - in particular, all manner of coloured shapes in three dimensions. What sort of head is it that, though containing innumerable sensations, is observed to lack eyes, ears, mouth, hair, and indeed all the bodily equipment which other heads are observed to contain? The plain fact is that this place must be kept clear of all such obstructions, of the slightest mistiness or colouring which could cloud my universe.

In any case, when I start groping around for my lost head, instead of finding it here I only lose my exploring hand as well: it, too, is swallowed up in the abyss at the centre of my being. Apparently this yawning cavern, this unoccupied base of all my operations, this nearest but virtually unknown region, this magical locality where I thought I kept my head, is in fact more like a beacon-fire so fierce that all things approaching it are instantly and utterly consumed, in order that its world-illuminating brilliance and clarity shall never for a moment be obscured. As for these lurking aches and tickles and so on, they can no more quench or shade this central brightness than these mountains and clouds and sky can do so. Quite the contrary: they all exist in its shining, and through them it is seen to shine. Present experience, whatever sense is employed, occurs only in an empty and absent head. For here and now my world and my head are incompatibles: they won't mix. There is no room for both at once on these shoulders, and fortunately it is my head with all its anatomy that has to go. This is not a matter of argument, or of philosophical acumen, or of working oneself up into a state, but of simple sight - of LOOK-WHO'S-HERE instead of IMAGINE-WHO'S-HERE, instead of TAKE-EVERYBODY-ELSE'S-WORD-FOR-WHO'S-HERE. If I fail to see what I am (and especially what I am not) it's because I'm too busily imaginative, too "spiritual", too adult and knowing, too credulous, too intimidated by society and language, too frightened of the obvious to accept the situation exactly as I find it at this moment. Only I am in a position to report on what's here. A kind of alert naïvety is what I need. It takes an innocent eye and an empty head (not to mention a stout heart) to admit their own perfect emptiness.

★　★　★　★　★　★

Probably there is only one way of converting the sceptic who still says I have a head here, and that is to invite him to come here and take a look for himself. But he must be an honest reporter, describing what he observes and nothing else.

Starting off on the far side of the room, he sees me as a full-length man-with-a-head. But as he approaches he finds half a man, then a head, then a blurred cheek or eye or nose, then a mere blur, and finally (at the point of contact) nothing at all. Alternatively, if he happens to be equipped with the necessary scientific instruments, he reports that the blur resolves itself into tissues, then cell-groups, then a single cell, a cell-nucleus, giant molecules... and so on, until he comes to a place where nothing is to be seen, to space which is empty of all solid or material objects. In either case, the observer who comes here to see what it's really like finds what I find here – vacancy. And if, having discovered and shared my nonentity here, he were to turn around (looking out with me instead of in at me) he would again find what I find – that this vacancy is filled to capacity with the scene. He, too, would find this central Point exploding into an Infinite Volume, this Nothing into the All, this Here into Everywhere.

And if my sceptical observer still doubts his senses, he may try his camera instead – a device which, lacking memory and anticipation, can register only what is contained in the place where it happens to be. It records the same impressions of me. Over there, it takes a man: midway, bits and pieces of the man: here, no man and nothing – or else, when pointed the other way round, his world.

★ ★ ★ ★ ★ ★

So *this* head is not a head, but a wrong-headed idea. If I can still find it here, I am "seeing things", and ought to hurry off to the doctor. It makes little difference whether I find my head, or Napoleon's, or the Virgin Mary's, or a fried egg, or a beautiful bunch of flowers: to have any topknot at all is to suffer from delusions.

During my lucid intervals, however, I am clearly headless here. Over there, on the other hand, I am clearly far from headless: indeed, I have more heads than I know what to do with.

Concealed in my human observers and in cameras, on display in picture frames, making faces behind shaving mirrors, peering out of door knobs and spoons and coffee pots and anything which will take a high polish, my heads are always turning up - though more-or-less shrunken and distorted, twisted back-to-front, often the wrong way up, and multiplied to infinity.

But there is one place where no head of mine can ever turn up, and that is here on my shoulders, where it would blot out this Central Void which is my very life-source: fortunately nothing is able to do that. In fact, these loose heads can never amount to more than impermanent and unprivileged accidents of that "outer" or phenomenal world which, though altogether one with the Central Essence, fails to affect it in the slightest degree. So unprivileged, indeed, is my head in the mirror, that I don't necessarily take it to be mine: as a very young child I didn't recognize myself in the glass, and neither do I now, when for a moment I regain my lost innocence. In my saner moments I see the man over there, the too-familiar fellow who lives in that other bathroom behind the looking-glass and seemingly spends all his time staring into this bathroom - that small, dull, circumscribed, particularized, ageing, and oh-so-vulnerable gazer - as the opposite in every way of my real Self here. I have never been anything but this ageless, measureless, lucid and altogether immaculate Void: it is unthinkable that I could ever have confused that staring wraith over there with what I plainly perceive myself to be here and now and always!

★　★　★　★　★　★

11

All this, however clearly given in first-hand experience, appears nevertheless wildly paradoxical, an affront to common-sense. Is it also an affront to science, which is said to be only common-sense tidied up somewhat? Anyhow, the scientist has his own story of how I see some things (such as your head) but not others (such as my head): and obviously his story works. The question is: can he put my head back on my shoulders, where people tell me it belongs?

At its briefest and plainest, his tale of how I see you runs something like this. Light leaves the sun, and eight minutes later gets to your body, which absorbs a part of it. The rest bounces off in all directions, and some of it reaches my eye, passing through the lens and forming an inverted picture of you on the screen at the back of my eyeball. This picture sets up chemical changes in a light-sensitive substance there, and these changes disturb the cells (they are tiny living creatures) of which the screen is built. They pass on their agitation to other, very elongated cells; and these, in turn, to cells in a certain region of my brain. It is only when this terminus is reached, and the molecules and atoms and particles of these brain-cells are affected, that I see you or anything else. And the same is true of the other senses; I neither see nor hear nor smell nor taste nor feel anything at all until the converging stimuli actually arrive, after the most drastic changes and delays, at this centre. It is only at this terminus, this moment and place of all arrivals at the Grand Central Station of my Here-Now, that the whole traffic

12

system – what I call my universe – springs into existence. For me, this is the time and place of all creation.

There are many odd things, infinitely remote from common-sense, about this plain tale of science. And the oddest of them is that the tale's conclusion cancels out the rest of it. For it says that all I can know is what is going on here and now, at this brain terminal, where my world is miraculously created. I have no way of finding out what is going on elsewhere – in the other regions of my head, in my eyes, in the outside world – if, indeed, there *is* an elsewhere, an outside world at all. The sober truth is that my body, and your body, and everything else on Earth, and the Universe itself – as they might exist out there in themselves and in their own space, independently of me – are mere figments, not worth a second thought. There neither is nor can be any evidence for two parallel worlds (an unknown outer or physical world there, plus a known inner or mental world here which mysteriously duplicates it) but only for this one world which is always before me, and in which I can find no division into mind and matter, inside and outside, soul and body. It is what it's observed to be, no more and no less, and it's the explosion of this centre – this terminal spot where "I" or "my consciousness" is supposed to be located – an explosion powerful enough to fill out and become this boundless scene that's now before me, that *is* me.

In brief, the scientist's story of perception, so far from contradicting my naïve story, only confirms it. Provisionally and common-sensibly, he put a head here on my shoulders, but it was soon ousted by the universe. The common-sense or un-paradoxical view of myself as an "ordinary man with a head" doesn't work at all; as soon as I examine it with any care, it turns out to be nonsense.

★ ★ ★ ★ ★ ★

And yet (I tell myself) it seems to work out well enough for all everyday, practical purposes. I carry on just as if there actually were, suspended here, plumb in the middle of my universe, a solid eight-inch ball. And I'm inclined to add that, in the uninquisitive and truly hard-headed world we all inhabit, this manifest absurdity can't be avoided: it is surely a fiction so convenient that it might as well be the plain truth.

In fact, it is always a lie, and often an inconvenient lie at that: it can even lose a person money. Consider, for instance, the designer of advertisements – whom nobody would accuse of

fanatical devotion to truth. His business is persuading me, and one of the most effective ways of doing that is to get me right into the picture as I really am. Accordingly he must leave my head out of it. Instead of showing the *other kind* of man – the one with a head – lifting a glass or a cigarette to his mouth, he shows *my kind* doing so: this right hand (held at precisely the correct angle in the bottom right-hand corner of the picture, and more-or-less armless) lifting a glass or a cigarette to – this no-mouth, this gaping void. *This* man is indeed no stranger, but myself as I am to myself. Almost inevitably I am involved. No wonder these bits and pieces of a body appearing in the corners of the picture, with no controlling mechanism of a head in the centre to connect or operate them – no wonder they look perfectly natural to me: I never had any other sort! And the ad-man's realism, his uncommon-sensical working knowledge of what I am really like, evidently pays off: when my head goes, my sales resistance is apt to follow. (However, there are limits: he is unlikely, for instance, to show a pink cloud just above the glass or the cigarette, because I supply that piece of realism anyhow. There would be no point in giving me another transparent nose-shadow.)

Film directors, also, are practical people, much more interested in the telling re-creation of experience than in discerning the nature of the experiencer; but in fact the one involves some of the other. Certainly these experts are well aware (for example) how feeble my reaction is to the sight of a vehicle obviously driven by someone else, compared with my reaction to the sight of a vehicle apparently driven by myself. In the first instance I am a spectator on the pavement, observing two similar cars swiftly approaching, colliding, killing the drivers, bursting into flames – and I am mildly interested. In the second, I am one of the drivers – headless, of course, like all first-person drivers, and my car (what little there is of it) is stationary. Here are my swaying knees, my foot hard down on the accelerator, my hands struggling with the steering wheel, the long bonnet sloping away in front, telephone poles whizzing by, the road snaking this way and that; and the other car, tiny at first, but looming larger and larger, coming straight at me, and then the crash, a great flash of light, and an empty silence... I sink back onto my seat and get my breath back. I have been taken for a ride.

How are they filmed, these first-person sequences? Two ways are possible: either a headless dummy is photographed, with camera in place of the head; or else a real man is photographed, with his head held far back or to one side to make room for the camera. In other words, so that I shall identify myself with the actor, his head is got out of the way: he must be my kind of person. For a picture of me-with-a-head is no likeness at all: it is a portrait of someone else, a case of mistaken identity.

It's curious that anyone should go to the advertising man for a glimpse into the deepest – and simplest – truths about himself; odd also that an elaborate modern invention like the cinema should help rid anyone of an illusion which very young children and animals are free of. But in other ages there were other and equally curious pointers to the all-too-obvious, and our human capacity for self-deception has surely never been complete. A profound though dim awareness of the human condition may well explain the popularity of many old cults and legends of loose and flying heads, or one-eyed or headless monsters and apparitions, of human bodies with non-human heads, and of martyrs who walked for miles after their heads were cut off – fantastic pictures, no doubt, but nearer than common-sense ever gets to a true portrait of *this* man, of the first person singular, present tense.

★ ★ ★ ★ ★ ★

My Himalayan experience, then, was no mere poetic fancy or airy mystical flight. In every way it turned out to be sober realism. And gradually, in the months and years that followed, the full extent of its practical implications and applications, its life-transforming consequences, dawned upon me.

For example, I saw that on two counts this new vision must transform my attitude to other men, and indeed to all creatures. Firstly, because it abolishes confrontation. Meeting you, there is for me only one face – yours – and I can never get face-to-face with you. In fact, we trade faces, and this is a most precious and intimate exchange of appearances. Secondly, because it gives me perfect insight into the Reality that lies behind your appearance, into you as you are for yourself, I have every reason to think the world of you. For I must believe that what is true for me is true for everyone, that we all are in the same condition – reduced to headless voids, to nothing, so that we may contain and become everything. That small, headed, solid-looking person I pass in the street – *that* one is the apparition which never stands up to close inspection, the heavily disguised one, the walking opposite and contradiction of the *real* one whose extent and content are infinite: and my respect for that person, as for every living thing, should be infinite too. His value and splendour cannot be overrated. Now I know exactly who he is and how to treat him.

In fact, he (or she) is myself. While we had a head apiece, obviously we were two. But now we are headless voids, what is there to part us? I can find no shell enclosing this void which I am, no shape or boundary or limit: so it cannot help but merge with other voids.

Of this merging I am my own perfect specimen. I don't doubt the scientist who says that, from his observation point over there, I have a clearly defined head consisting of an immense hierarchy of clearly defined bodies such as organs, cells, and molecules – an inexhaustibly complex world of physical things and processes. But I happen to know (or rather, to be) the inside story of this world and every one of its inhabitants, and it completely contradicts the outside story. Right here, I find that every member of this vast community, from the smallest particle to my head itself, has vanished like darkness in sunlight. No outsider is qualified to speak for them: only I am in a position to do so, and I swear they are all lucid, simple, empty, and one, without trace of division.

If this is true of my head, it is equally true of everything I take to be "myself" and "here" – in brief, of this total body-mind. What is it really like (I ask myself) where I am, now? Am I shut up in what Marcus Aurelius called this bag of blood and corruption (and what we might call this walking zoo, or cell-city, or chemical factory, or cloud of particles), or am I shut out of it? Do I spend my life embedded inside a solid, man-shaped block (roughly six feet by two by one), or outside that block, or perhaps both inside and outside it? The fact is: things aren't like that at all. There are no obstructions here, no inside or outside, no room or lack of room, no hiding place or shelter: I can find no home here to live in or to be locked out of, and not an inch of ground to build it on. But this homelessness suits me perfectly – a void needs no housing. In short, this physical order of things, so solid-looking in appearance and at a distance, is always soluble without residue on really close inspection.

And I find this is true, not only of my human body, but of my total Body, the universe itself. (Even from the outsider's viewpoint, the distinction between these embodiments is an artificial one: this little body is so united functionally to all other things, so dependent upon its environment, that it is non-existent and unthinkable by itself; in fact, no creature can survive for a moment except as that one Body which alone is all there, self-contained, independent, and therefore truly alive.) How much of this total Body I take on depends upon the occasion, but automatically I feel my way into as much as I need. Thus I may with perfect ease identify myself in turn with my head, my six-foot body, my family, my country, my planet and solar system (as when I imagine them threatened by others) – and so on, without ever coming up against any limit or barrier. And however great or small my temporary embodiment – this part of the world that I call mine and take to be here, that I am now thinking and feeling for, that I have for backing, whose point of view I have adopted, into whose shoes I put myself – it invariably turns out to be void, nothing here in itself. The reality behind all appearances is lucid, open, and altogether accessible. I know my way in and out of the secret inmost heart of every creature, however remote or repulsive it might seem to the outsider, because we all are one Body, and that Body is one Void.

And that Void is *this* void, complete and indivisible, not shared out or split up into mine and yours and theirs, but all of it present here and now. This very spot, this observation-post of mine, this particular "hole where a head should have been" - *this* is the Ground and Receptacle of all existence, the one Source of all that appears (when projected "over there") as the physical or phenomenal world, the one infinitely fertile Womb from which all creatures are born and into which they all return. It is absolutely Nothing, yet all things; the only Reality, yet an absentee. It is my Self. There is nothing else whatever. I am everyone and no-one, and Alone.

The soul has now no further awareness of the body and will give herself no foreign name, not man, not living being, nor anything at all.

PLOTINUS

After the body has been cast off to a distance like a corpse, the Sage never more attaches himself to it.

SANKARA

If one opens one's eyes and seeks the body, it is not to be found any more. This is called: In the empty chamber it grows light. Inside and outside, everything is equally light. That is a very favourable sign.
The Secret of the Golden Flower

Vow to achieve the perfect understanding that the illusory body is like dew and lightning.
Zen master Hsu Yun (on his death-bed, in 1959)

3
Discovering Zen

In the months and years that followed my original experience of headlessness, then, I tried very hard to understand it, with the results that I have briefly described. The character of the vision itself didn't change during this period, though it tended to come more easily when invited, and to stay longer. But its working out, its meaning, developed as it went along, and was of course much influenced by my reading. Some help and encouragement I certainly found in books – scientific, philosophical, and religious. In particular, I found that some of the mystics seemed to have seen and valued what I see myself to be, here.

Discussion, on the other hand, proved almost invariably quite fruitless. "Naturally I can't see my head," my friends would say. "So what?" And foolishly I would begin to reply: "So everything! So you and the whole world are turned upside down and inside out..." It was no good. I was unable to describe my experience in a way that interested the hearers, or conveyed to them anything of its quality or significance. They really had no idea what I was talking about – for both sides an embarrassing situation. Here was something perfectly obvious, immensely significant, a revelation of pure and astonished delight – to me and nobody else! When people start seeing things others can't see, eyebrows are raised, doctors sent for. And here was I in much the same condition, except that mine was a case of *not* seeing things. Some loneliness and frustration were inevitable. This is how a real madman must feel (I thought) - cut off, unable to communicate.

An added reason for dismay was the fact that, among my acquaintances, it was often the more cultivated and intelligent who seemed specially unable to see the point: as if headlessness were an infantile aberration which, like thumb-sucking, one should have grown out of and forgotten long ago. As for writers, some of the most brilliant positively went out of their way to tell me I was crazy - or else they were. Chesterton, in *The Napoleon of Notting Hill*, ends his ironic list of science-fiction wonders with the crowning absurdity: men without heads! And the great philosopher Descartes (justly reckoned great because he starts his revolutionary inquiry by asking what is clearly given) goes one better: he actually begins his list of certainties - of things which are "true because perceived by the senses" - with the astonishing announcement: "Firstly, I perceived that I had a head." Even the man in the street, who should know better, says of something particularly obvious: "Why, it's as plain as the nose on your face!" With all the world of obvious things to choose from, he had to pick that!

I still preferred the evidence of my own senses to all hear-say. If this was madness, at least it wasn't second-hand madness. In any case, I never doubted that what I saw was what the mystics saw. Only the odd thing was that so few seemed to have seen it quite this way. Most of the masters of the spiritual life appeared to have "kept their heads"; or if not, few thought the loss worth mentioning. And certainly none of them, so far as I could discover, included the practice of headlessness in any curriculum of spiritual exercises. Why was such an obvious pointer, such a convincing and ever-present demonstration of that Nothingness which spiritual teachers never tire of proclaiming, so neglected?

After all, it's absurdly obvious; there's no escaping it. If anything hits you in the face, this does. I was puzzled: even, at times, discouraged.

And then – better late than never – I stumbled upon Zen.

★　★　★　★　★　★

Zen Buddhism has the reputation of being difficult – and almost impossibly so for Westerners, who for this reason are often advised to stick to their own religious tradition if they can. My own experience has been exactly the other way round. At last, after more than a decade of largely fruitless searching everywhere else, I found in the words of the Zen masters many echoes of the central experience of my life: they talked my language, spoke to my condition. Many of these masters, I found, had not only lost their heads (as we all have) but were vividly aware of their condition and its immense significance, and used every device to bring their disciples to the same realization. Let me give a few examples.

The famous *Heart Sutra,* which summarizes the essence of Mahayana Buddhism and is daily recited in Zen monasteries, having begun by stating that the body is just emptiness, declares that there is no eye, no ear, no nose. Understandably, this bald pronouncement perplexed the young Tung-shan (807–869); and his teacher, who was not a Zenist, also failed to make much of it. The pupil surveyed the teacher carefully, then explored his own face with his fingers. "You have a pair of eyes," he protested, "and a pair of ears, and the rest; and so have I. Why does the Buddha tell us there are no such things?" His teacher replied: "I can't help you. You must be trained by a Zen master." He went off and took this advice. However, his question remained unanswered till, years later, he happened while out walking to look down into a pool of still water. There he discovered those human features the

Buddha was talking about - on show where they belonged, where he had always kept them: over there at a distance, leaving this place forever transparent, forever clean of them, as of everything else. This simplest of discoveries - this revelation of the perfectly obvious - turned out to be the essential realization that Tung-shan had been seeking for so long, and it led to his becoming not just a noted Zen master himself, but the founder of Soto, which is today Zen's largest sect.

A century or more before this incident, Hui-neng (637-712), the Sixth Patriarch of Zen, had given his famous piece of advice on the same subject. He counselled his brother-monk Ming to call a halt to all his craving and cogitation, and *see:* "See what at this very moment your own face looks like - the Face you had before you (and indeed your parents) were born." It is recorded that Ming thereupon discovered within himself that fundamental source of all things which hitherto he had sought outside. Now he understood the whole matter, and found himself bathed in tears and sweat. Saluting the Patriarch, he asked what other secrets remained to uncover. "In what I have shown you," replied Hui-neng, "there is nothing hidden. If you look within and recognize your own 'Original Face', all secrets are in you."

Hui-neng's Original Face (No-face, No-thing at all) is the best known and for many the most helpful of all Zen koan-anecdotes: over the centuries in China it is said to have proved a uniquely effective pointer to enlightenment. In fact, according to Daito Kokushi (1281-1337), all the seventeen hundred koans of Zen are simply pointers to our Original and Featureless Face. Of it, Mumon (13th c.) says:

> You cannot describe it or draw it,[*]
> You cannot praise it enough or perceive it.

[*] But you can indicate it in a drawing - see page 2 - or rather, outside the drawing, by what's missing from it.

No place can be found in which to put the Original Face;
It will not disappear even when the universe is
destroyed.

One of Hui-neng's successors, the Zen master Shih-t'ou (700–790), took a slightly different line. "Do away with your throat and lips, and let me hear what you can say," he commanded. A monk replied: "I have no such things!" "Then you may enter the gate," was the encouraging reply. And there's a very similar story of a contemporary of Shih-t'ou's, master Pai Chang (720–814), who asked one of his monks how he managed to speak without throat, lips, or tongue. It is, of course, from the silent Void that one's voice issues – from the Void of which Huang-po (d. 850) writes: "It is all-pervading, spotless beauty; it is the self-existent and uncreated Absolute. Then how can it even be a matter for discussion that the real Buddha has no mouth and preaches no Dharma, or that real hearing requires no ears, for who could hear it? Ah, it is a jewel beyond all price."

As an aid to such a realization, Bodhidharma, the First Patriarch of Zen (6th c.) is said to have prescribed a good hammer-blow on the back of the head. Tai-hui (1089–1163) was equally uncompromising: "This matter (Zen) is like a great mass of fire: when you approach it your face is sure to be scorched. It is again like a sword about to be drawn; when it is once out of the scabbard, someone is sure to lose his life... The precious vajra sword is right here and its purpose is to cut off the head." Indeed this beheading was a common topic of conversation between Zen master and pupil. For instance, this 9th century exchange:

Lung-ya: If I threatened to cut off your head with the
sharpest sword in the world, what would you do?
The master pulled in his head.
Lung-ya: Your head is off!
The master smiled.

Evidently master and pupil, both headless, understood each other well. How well, also, they would have understood the advice of the Muslim Jalalu'l-Din Rumi, Persia's foremost mystical poet (1207–1273): "Behead yourself!" "Dissolve your whole body into Vision: become seeing, seeing, seeing!"

"I have learned from Him," says another great mystical poet, the Indian Kabir (b.1440), "to see without eyes, to hear without ears, to drink without mouth."

However could Kabir see, if he had no eyes to see with? Well, as we have already noted, modern science itself agrees that we don't really see with our eyes. They are merely links in a long chain stretching from the sun, through sunlight and atmosphere and illuminated objects, through eye lenses and retinae and optic nerves, right down to particle/wavicle-haunted space in a region of the brain, where at last (it's said) seeing really occurs. In fact, the deeper the physiologist probes into the object, the nearer he gets to the Emptiness which is the Subject's direct experience of himself – the Emptiness which is the only Seer and Hearer, the sole Experiencer. (Not that he can ever, no matter how refined his instruments and techniques, get to the Subject by probing into the object: to do that he has simply to turn his attention round 180°.) And this lines up perfectly with what the old Zen masters say. "The body," Rinzai (d.867) tells us, "does not know how to discourse or to listen to a discourse... This which is unmistakably peceivable right where you are, absolutely identifiable yet without form – this is what listens to the discourse." Here the Chinese master, along with Kabir and the rest, is echoing the *Surangama Sutra* (a pre-Zen Indian scripture) which teaches that it's absurd to suppose that we see with our eyes, or hear with our ears: it's because these have melted together, and vanished into the absolute Emptiness of our "original bright and charming Face", that experience of any sort is possible.

Still earlier, the Taoist sage Chuang-tzu (c.300 B.C.) draws a delightful picture of this featureless Face or empty head of mine. He calls it "Chaos, the Sovereign of the Centre", and contrasts its utter blankness here with those familiar seven-holed heads out there: "Fuss, the god of the Southern Ocean, and Fret, the god of the Northern Ocean, happened once to meet in the realm of Chaos, the god of the Centre. Chaos treated them very handsomely and they discussed together what they could do to repay his kindness. They had noticed that, whereas everyone else has seven apertures, for sight, hearing, eating, breathing, Chaos had none. So they decided to make the experiment of boring holes in him. Every day they bored a hole, and on the seventh day Chaos died."

No matter how much I fuss and fret, and renew my attempts to murder the Sovereign of the Centre by superimposing my human seven-holed features upon him, I can never succeed. The mask out there in the mirror can never touch my Original Face here, much less disfigure It. No shadow can fall upon Chaos, the unbodied and eternal King.

✷　✷　✷　✷　✷　✷

But why all this emphasis on the disappearance of the face and head, rather than of the body as a whole? The answer is plain for humans to see. (Crocodiles and crabs would have a different story to tell!) For me here the face with its sense organs happens to be quite special in that it's *always* absent, always absorbed in this immense Void which I am; whereas my trunk and arms and legs are sometimes similarly absorbed and sometimes not. How much the Void currently includes, and excludes, is unimportant: for I see that it remains infinitely empty and infinitely big regardless of the scope or importance of the finite objects it's taking care of. It makes no real difference whether it's dissolving my head (as when I look down), or my human body (as when I look out), or my Earth-body (as when, out-of-doors, I look up), or my Universe-body (as when I close my eyes). Everything there, no matter how tiny or vast, is equally soluble here, equally capable of coming and showing me that I am no-thing here.

In the literature we find many eloquent accounts of the dissolution of the whole body. I quote a few examples.

Yengo (1566–1642) writes of Zen: "It is presented right to your face, and at this moment the whole thing is handed over to you... Look into your whole being... Let your body and mind be turned into an inanimate object of nature like a stone or a piece of wood; when a state of perfect motionlessness and unawareness is obtained all the signs of life will depart and also every trace of limitation will vanish. Not a single idea will disturb your consciousness, when lo! all of a sudden you will come to realize a light abounding in full gladness. It is like coming across a light in thick darkness; it is like receiving treasure in poverty. The four elements and the five aggregates (your entire bodily make-up) are no more felt as burdens; so light, so easy, so free you are. Your very existence has been delivered from all limitations; you have become open, light, and transparent. You gain an illuminating insight into the very nature of things, which now appear to you as so many fairy-like flowers having no graspable reality. Here is manifested the unsophisticated self which is the Original Face of your being; here is shown all bare the most beautiful landscape of your birthplace. There is but one straight passage open and unobstructed through and through. This is where you surrender all – your body, your life, and all that belongs to your inmost self. This is where you gain peace, ease, non-doing, and inexpressible delight."

The characteristic lightness which Yengo refers to was experienced by the Taoist Lieh-tzu (c.400 B.C.) to such a degree that he seemed to be riding on the wind. This is how he describes the feeling: "Internal and external were blended into a unity. After that, there was no distinction between eye and ear, ear and nose, nose and mouth: all were the same. My mind was frozen, my body in dissolution, my flesh and bones all melted together. I was wholly unconscious of what my body was resting on, or what was under my feet. I was borne this way and that on the wind, like dry chaff or leaves falling from a tree. In fact, I knew not whether the wind was riding on me or I on the wind."

The 16th-century Zen master Han-shan says of the enlightened man that his body and heart are entirely non-existent: they are the same as the absolute Void. Of his own experience he writes: "I took a walk. Suddenly I stood still, filled with the realization that I had no body or mind. All I could see was one great illuminating Whole – omnipresent, perfect, lucid, and serene. It was like an all-embracing mirror from which the mountains and rivers of the earth were projected... I felt clear and transparent." "Mind and body dropped off!" exclaims Dogen (1200-1253) in an ecstasy of release. "Dropped off! Dropped off! This state must be experienced by you all; it is like piling fruit into a basket without a bottom, it is like pouring water into a bowl with a hole in it." "All of a sudden you find your mind and body wiped out of existence," says Hakuin (1685-1768): "This is what is known as letting go your hold. As you regain your breath it is like drinking water and knowing it is cold. It is joy inexpressible."

In our own century, D.T. Suzuki sums up the matter: "To Zen, incarnation is excarnation; the flesh is no-flesh; here-now equals emptiness *(sunyata)* and infinity." Outside Zen, it's not easy to find statements quite so clear, and so free from religiosity, as this. However, many parallels can be found in other traditions, as soon as one knows what to look for. This is only to be expected: the essential vision must transcend the accidents of history and geography.

Inevitably the closest parallel is to be found in India, the original home of Buddhism. Sankara (c.820), the great sage and interpreter of Advaita or absolute non-duality, taught that a man has no hope of liberation until he ceases to identify himself with the body, which is a mere illusion born of ignorance: his real Self is like space, unattached, pure, infinite. Confusing the unreal body with this real Self is bondage and misery. This doctrine still survives in India. One of its most lucid recent exemplars, Ramana Maharshi (1879-1950), would say to inquirers: "Till now you seriously considered yourself to be the body and to have a form. That is the primal ignorance which is the root cause of all trouble."

Nor is Christianity (though, as Archbishop Temple observed, it is the most materialistic of the great religions) unaware of the fact that genuine illumination must dispel the dark opacity of our bodies no less than of our souls. "When thine eye is single," said Jesus mysteriously, "thy whole body also is full of light." This single eye is surely identical with the precious Third Eye of Indian mysticism, which enables the seer simultaneously to look in at his Emptiness and out at what's filling it. And the same, also, as the priceless gem which (according to Eastern tradition) we search everywhere for but here on our foreheads, where we all wear it.

Augustine Baker (1575-1641) writes of the Christian contemplative: "At length he cometh to a pure and total abstraction; and then he seemeth to himself to be all spirit and as if he had no body... The purer and perfecter such abstraction is, the higher is the man ascended to perfection." This is a comment upon a well-known passage in *The Cloud of Unknowing*, a 14th-century mystical work which teaches that a vivid awareness of our non-existence is the prerequisite of true joy: for "all men have matter for sorrow: but most specially he feeleth matter of sorrow that knoweth and feeleth that he *is*." But of course this indispensable self-naughting is a favourite theme of all Christian mysticism. No one describes its two sides more boldly than St. Bernard (1091–1153): "It is no merely human joy to lose oneself like this, so to be emptied of oneself as though one almost ceased to be at all; it is the bliss of heaven... How otherwise could God be 'all in all', if anything of man remained in man?"

Sometimes in the West, even the mystic's language is as Zen-like as what it describes. Gerlac Peterson (1378–1411), speaks of a "showing" that is "so vehement and so strong that the whole of the interior man, not only of his heart but of his body, is marvellously moved and shaken... His interior aspect is made clear without any cloud." His spiritual eye is wide open. Instead of remaining, as Shakespeare puts it,

Most ignorant of what he's most assured,

His glassy essence,

- and therefore behaving like an angry ape - he sees into its utmost depths, into the transparent heart of Reality.

With our attention fastened upon the physical world, we fail to see through it. Disregarding our inside information, we look on our little human bodies as opaque and divided from our total Body, the Universe, which as a result seems equally opaque and divided. Some of our poets, however, are not so tricked and taken in by (so-called) common sense, but instead take in all things and revel in their transparency. Rainer Maria Rilke wrote of his dead friend:

For these, these shadowy vales and waving grasses

And streams of running water were his face,

but didn't stop with dissolving the human face and human body: his declared mission was to go on and "render the earth we live on, and by extension the universe, invisible, and thus to transform it into a higher plane of reality." For Rilke, this ever-present Void, our undying Face, has no boundaries. As Traherne says of himself:

The sense itself was I.
I felt no dross nor matter in my soul,
No brims nor borders, such as in a bowl
We see. My essence was capacity.

And, in a better-known passage: "You never enjoy the world aright, till the sea itself floweth in your veins, till you are clothed with the heavens, and crowned with the stars."

This is none other than the Zen experience of satori - only the language differs a little. At the moment of satori there is an explosion, and a man has no body but the universe. "He feels his body and mind, the earth and the heavens, fuse into one pellucid whole - pure, alert, and wide-awake," says master Po Shan:

The whole earth is but one of my eyes,
But a spark of my illuminating light.

In numerous texts we are told how the enlightened man as if by magic engulfs rivers, mountains, seas, the great world itself, reducing them all to the Void here, to nothing at all; and then, out of this Void, creates rivers, mountains, seas, the great world itself. Without the slightest discomfort, he swallows all the water in the West River, and spews it up again. He takes in and abolishes all things, produces all things. He sees the universe as nothing else than the outflowing of his own profound Nature, which in itself remains unstained, absolutely transparent. Now he is restored to himself as he really is: as the very heart of existence, from which all being is made manifest. In brief, he is deified. Established at the unique Source, he cries: "I am the Centre, I am the Universe, I am the Creator!" (D.T. Suzuki) Or: "I am the cause of mine own self and all things!" (Eckhart) In the vivid language of Zen, the mangy cur has become the golden-haired lion roaring in the desert, spontaneous, free, energetic, magnificently self-sufficient, and alone. Arrived Home at last, he finds no room for two. Our own Traherne once more echoes Eastern masters when he exclaims: "The streets were mine, the temple was mine, the people were mine, their clothes and gold and silver were mine, as much as their sparkling eyes, fair skins and ruddy faces. The skies were mine, and so were the sun and moon and stars, and all the World was mine: and I the only spectator and enjoyer of it."

What I call perfection of seeing is not seeing others but oneself.

CHAUANG-TZU (3rd c. B.C.)

Seeing into Nothingness – this is the true seeing, the eternal seeing.

SHEN-HUI (8th c.)

He who knows that he is Spirit, becomes Spirit, becomes everything; neither gods nor men can prevent him...
The gods dislike people who get this knowledge...
The gods love the obscure and hate the obvious.

BRIHADARANYAKA UPANISHAD (7th c. B.C.)

The foolish reject what they see, not what they think; the wise reject what they think, not what they see...
Observe things as they are and don't pay attention to other people.

HUANG-PO (9th c.)

To one who knows nothing, It is clearly revealed.

MEISTER ECKHART (1260–1327)

And what rule do you think I walked by? Truly a strange one, but the best in the whole world. I was guided by an implicit faith in God's goodness; and was therefore led to the study of the most obvious and common things.

THOMAS TRAHERNE (1627–1674)

He who doubts from what he sees
Will ne'er believe, do what you please.

WILLIAM BLAKE (1757–1827)

The aspects of things that are most important for us are hidden because of their simplicity and familiarity.

LUDWIG WITTGENSTEIN (1889–1951)

This is it. There are no hidden meanings. All that mystical stuff is just what's so.

WERNER ERHARD (1935-   )

The purloined letter, in Edgar Allan Poe's story (1845), "escaped observation by being excessively obvious." The villain "deposited the letter immediately beneath the nose of the whole world, by way of best preventing any portion of the world perceiving it."

4
Bringing the story up to date

The eight stages of the Headless Way

It is over forty years since the initial "Himalayan" experience came out of the blue, and over twenty since the foregoing description of it was first published. They have been full years - a time of many surprises and some shocks - during which the experience has of itself opened out into a Path (the Headless Way is as good a name for it as any), and much has been learned about this Path - its twists and turns and traffic flow and traffic blocks, its general practicability. A map of it all, from the very beginning (long before the "Himalayan" vision), is long overdue.

This concluding chapter attempts such a map. It represents, of course, just one of the countless variations on that archetypal Way which leads (in the words of the *Brihadaranyaka Upanishad*) "from the unreal to the Real, from darkness to Light, from death to Immortality." Here and there it lines up and merges with the Way of Zen; elsewhere it strikes out on its own. If it seems more straightforward and easier going than that ancient and Far Eastern Way, that's because it takes us through the familiar landscape of contemporary Western culture, not because it's shorter or

35

smoother. It isn't. Not, of course, that our detailed routing will suit all Western travellers. Except for the first three stages (which we all pass through) our map is - it has to be - modelled on the author's own itinerary. The extent to which it coincides with the reader's is for the reader to determine. There are bound to be divergences, even huge ones. But at least the earlier stages of our sketch-map will indicate how far he's already come, and the later ones will give him some idea of what he's in for - the landmarks and staging posts, the side-tracks and pitfalls, which he's likely to come across - if he should find himself pursuing the Headless Way.

All Ways are divisible into more-or-less arbitrary and often overlapping stages. Here, we distinguish eight: (1) The Headless Infant, (2) The Child, (3) The Headed Grown-up, (4) The Headless Seer, (5) Practising Headlessness, (6) Working It Out, (7) The Barrier, (8) The Breakthrough.

(1) The Headless Infant

As an infant you were like any animal: in that you were *for yourself* headless and faceless and eyeless, immense, at large, unseparate from your world - without being aware of your blessed condition. Unconsciously, you lived without obstruction from What you are Where you are, from your Source, and relied simply on the Given. What was presented to you really was *present* - the Moon was no bigger or further off than the hand that clutched at it. Your world really was *your* world - distance, that most plausible and rapacious of sneak-thieves, hadn't begun to filch it from you. The obvious really was *obvious* - the rattle that fell out of sight no longer existed: disappearance meant annihilation. You made no claim to that face in your mirror. It stayed there: it was that baby's, not yours.

(2) The Child

Gradually you learned the fateful and essential art of going out and looking back at yourself, as if from a few feet away and through others' eyes, and "seeing" yourself from their point of view as a human being like them, with a normal head on your shoulders. Normal yet unique. You came to identify with that particular face in your mirror, and answer to its name. Yet you remained *for yourself* at large, headless, boundless Space for your world to happen in. In fact it's likely that at times you became well aware of that Space. (A child is apt to ask why others have heads and he hasn't, or declare that he's nothing, not present, invisible. Carlos, at his third birthday party, when asked to locate various aunts and uncles, pointed to each in turn correctly. Then someone asked him where Carlos was. He waved his hands aimlessly: Carlos could not locate Carlos. On a later occasion, when rebuked for being a naughty boy, he didn't object to being called *naughty,* but protested he was not a *boy.* Soon after, he went to his grandmother and announced that he *was* a boy!)

At this stage you come near to making the best of both worlds – the unlimited non-human world you are coming from and the limited human world you are entering. All-too-briefly, you have in effect *two* identities going, two versions of yourself. For private purposes you are still no-thing, spaced out, vast, extending even to the stars (though now far away, you are quite capable of including them: they are still *your* stars): while for social purposes you are increasingly the opposite of all this. If we adults have to become like little ones in order to enter the Kingdom of Heaven, it is like little ones of this happy age (up to five years, say) that we will do so – little ones who are for themselves big ones, who are still immense, more truly grown-up than the grown-ups, so-called.

(3) The Headed Grown-up

Humans develop, however, at amazingly different rates. Poppy, as early as two years, was already much given to contemplating herself in the mirror: and, at two years three months, when her mother (I think unwisely) suggested there might be no face or just emptiness on the near side of the mirror - right where she was - she replied: "Don't talk about it, it frightens me!" It seems that, from a very early age, our learned view of ourselves from outside begins to overshadow, to superimpose itself upon, and eventually to blot out, our original view of ourselves from inside. We have grown down, not up. Instead of being present and together with the stars - and all things under the stars - we have shrunk away and withdrawn from them. Instead of containing our world, it now contains us - what's left of us. And so, reduced from being the whole scene into being this tiny part, is it any wonder if you and I find ourselves in all sorts of trouble - if we grow greedy, resentful, alienated, frightened, defeated, tired, stiff, imitative instead of creative, unloving, plain crazy? Or, in more detail:

Greedy - as we try to regain and accumulate at any cost as much as possible of our lost empire,

Resentful or aggressive - as we seek revenge on a social order that has cruelly cut us down to size,

Alienated, lonely, suspicious - because we morbidly imagine that people, and even animals and inanimate objects, keep their distance from us, are aloof and stand-offish: and we refuse to see how that distance folds to nothing, so that in reality they are right with us here, our bosom companions and intimates, closer than close,

Frightened - as we see ourselves to be things, at the mercy of and up against all other things,

Defeated - because working for this individual something is

making sure of failure: the probable end of even our most "successful" enterprises is disillusion, the certain end is death,

Tired - because the building and maintenance and constant adjustment of this imaginary box for living in, right here, uses up so much energy,

Stiff, solemn, unnatural, phony - because we're living from a lie, and from a lumpish, inflexible, predictable, petty, limiting lie, at that,

Uncreative - because we cut ourselves off from our Source and Centre and see ourselves as a mere regional effect,

Unloving - because we shut all others out from the volume we imagine we occupy, pretending we are not built open, not built for loving,

Crazy - because we "see" things that aren't present, and actually believe (contrary to all the evidence) that we are at 0 metres what we look like at 2 metres - solid, opaque, coloured, outlined lumps of stuff. How can our life and our world stay sane if their very Centre has gone insane?

Insofar as we don't suffer from these multiple handicaps we remain "little children at heart" at Stage (2), headless, transparent, lightsome, and more or less unconsciously in touch with the truth of what we are. Or else we have already moved on to a much later stage. In any case, the fundamental reason why so many of us get by, and don't fall chronically ill or go raving mad, is both simple and reassuring. If, in our day-to-day lives, we are quite often sensible, loving, generous, laughter-filled, and even happy, that is because all of us - at whatever stage we happen to have arrived - are rooted in and living from our common Source and central Perfection, from one and the same Headlessness, or Original Face or Transparency or Aware Nothingness. All along we are fully enlightened by one and the same Inner Light, whether we let it shine through or not. Our happiness is deep-rooted and real, while our misery is shallow-rooted and unreal, born of delusion, of ignorance. We suffer because we overlook the fact that, at heart, we are all right.

Which prompts the question: is Stage (3) – this stretch of road so paved with delusion-based suffering – just a great mistake, an unnecessary loop which can and should be by-passed? It is possible to leap – helped on by enlightened parents and teachers – from the childhood of Stage (2) to the true adulthood or seership of later stages, thus avoiding the worst of the troubles we have just listed? In other words, can one become a full member of this club called Human Society, and enjoy its inestimable privileges and facilities, yet without ever subscribing to the lie on which it is founded, without ever joining in the club's non-stop Face Game,* without ever becoming *like them*? Rilke, writing of a poignant incident in his childhood, wasn't hopeful. "But then the worst happens. They take him by the hand and draw him towards the table; and all of them, as many as are there present, gather inquisitively before the lamp. They have the best of it; they keep in the shadow, while on him falls, with the light, *all the shame of having a face.* Shall he stay and pretend to live the sort of life they ascribe to him, and grow to resemble them...?"†

The question we are asking is whether we can refuse these imaginary top-knots *(mot juste!)*, these shameful and (insofar as they "take") these malignant growths which society is deter-

---

* *The Face Game* (by D.E. Harding, in *Transactional Analysis Bulletin,* April, 1967) regards the innumerable and often desperate "games people play" as branches stemming from this Game of games. Cutting them back here and there may only make them grow more vigorously elsewhere. To get rid of them all and become game-free, sever the parent trunk, which is the pretence that there's somebody here to play games – a person (*persona,* mask), a face right here where I am, confronting your face there, face-to-face, partner-to-partner, in a symmetrical (and therefore game-playing) relationship.

† *The Notebooks of Malte Laurids Brigge,* trans. John Linton, Hogarth, London, 1959. The italics are not in the original.

mined to implant and cultivate right here on our own shoulders –
and all that those growths involve?

The answer is: in practice, No. There is no opting out, no short
cut. We have to take on that burden and travel that long loop in
the road. It's true that a few do decline to do so, and never come
to view themselves from a distance as second or third persons.
Somewhat like the elder brother in the story of the Prodigal Son,
they stay at Home being first-person-singular, present tense, in
all innocence. It's not a state to be envied. Unable to conceive and
come to terms with how others see them, they are labelled
"retardates" or worse, are apt to behave accordingly, and to need
institutional care. In fact, there's no route from the Paradise of
childhood to the Heaven of the blessed that doesn't lie through
the Far Country, through some kind of Hell or at least Purgatory.
Really to turn away from our wilfulness, to abandon our personal
and separative ego (and so come to the later stages of our
journey) we must at this stage be paid-up members of the society
which is dedicated to their cultivation: as small children our
egocentricity is as yet too shallow, too ineffectual and variable
and candid, too little ours, for us to give up. Really to lose our
heads, we must first have them firmly in place. Really to appreci-
ate What we are, with clarity and impact, we must first be identified with what we are not. Really to value the perfectly obvious,
we must first acquire the habit of overlooking and denying it. The
Universe is such that true liberation doesn't happen *in vacuo:* it is
liberation from what's false – without which it isn't liberation at
all. So it comes about that our list of troubles – that alas-far-from-
complete tale of woe – isn't all woe. It is the precondition of a free-
dom that can be had no other way. It contributes hugely and
essentially to that realization – that re-discovery of the obvious –
which eventually overcomes it, which is its cure in general and in
detail. It underlies that ultimate bliss which (as we shall see) may

be found towards the end of our journey. Meanwhile our troubles certainly provide the strongest of motives for pressing on. Who would want to be held up for longer than necessary in this painful region? And who, having already made such progress along the Way, would not want to continue – specially as our next stage is by far the easiest and most straightforward of them all?

(4) The Headless Seer

All one has to do to enter this Fourth Stage of the journey is – however briefly – to turn round the arrow of one's attention. The *Katha Upanishad* puts it this way: "God made the senses turn outwards, man therefore looks outwards, not into himself. But occasionally a daring soul, desiring immortality, has looked back and found himself." In fact the "daring soul" doesn't lack encouragement. He's surrounded by countless reminders and opportunities, countless means of reversing the arrow of attention – if only he's sufficiently inquisitive about his true identity, and *if only he's willing to drop for a moment opinions about himself based on hearsay and memory and imagination, and to rely on PRESENT EVIDENCE.*

Here are three of the many means of making the turnabout, for the attentive and honest reader instantly to try out:

(i) What you are now looking *at* is this printing; what you are now looking *out of* is empty Space for this printing. Trading your head for it, you put nothing in its way: you vanish in its favour.

(ii) What you are now looking out of isn't two small and tightly fastened "windows" called eyes but one immense and wide open "Window" without any edges; in fact you *are* this frameless, glassless "Window".

(iii) To make quite sure of this, you have only to point to the "Window" and notice what that finger is pointing at – if anything. Please do just that, now...

Contrary, no doubt, to one's first impression, conscious headlessness or transparency – this seeing into the Nothingness-right-where-one-is – turns out to have several unique virtues. *There's no experience at all like it.* Here are just five of its peculiarities – not for the reader to believe, but to verify:

First, though down the centuries this in-seeing has been made out to be the most difficult thing in the world, the joke is that it is really the easiest. This pious confidence trick has taken in countless earnest seekers. The treasure of treasures they wore themselves out searching for is in fact the most accessible, the most exposed and blatantly obvious of finds, lit up and on show all the time. The Buddha's description of Nirvana, in the Pali Canon, as "visible in this life, inviting, attractive, accessible," is clearly true and makes perfect sense. So does Master Ummon's statement that the *first* step along the Zen Path is to see into our Void Nature: getting rid of our bad *karma* comes after – not before – that seeing. So does Ramana Maharshi's insistence that it is easier to see What and Who we really are than to see "a gooseberry in the palm of our hand" – as so often, this Hindu sage confirms Zen teaching. All of which means there are no preconditions for this essential in-seeing. To oneself one's Nature is forever clearly displayed, and it's amazing how one could ever pretend otherwise. It's available now, just as one is, and doesn't require the seer to be holy, or learned, or clever, or special in any way. Rather the reverse! What a superb advantage and opportunity this is!

Second, this alone is real seeing. It can't be done wrong, and is

43

quite foolproof. Look and see now whether it's possible to be *more-or-less* headless, to perceive partially or dimly the Emptiness where you are. This seeing of the *Subject* is a perfect and all-or-nothing experience, compared with which the seeing of *objects* (such as this page covered with black marks, and the hands holding it, and their background) is mere glimpsing: a very great deal of the scene is missed, just not registered. The view out is never clear, the view in never foggy – as Chuang-tzu and Shen-hui imply in the quotations prefacing this chapter.

Third, this seeing goes deep. The clearest and most distant of views *out* is found to be shallow – a view down a cul-de-sac – compared with the view *in,* to the headlessness which plainly goes on and on forever. We could describe it as penetrating to the inmost depths of our conscious Nature, and beyond them to the Abyss beyond consciousness itself, beyond even existence, but this is really too complicated and wordy. What a vista of transparency opens out – or rather, *in* – when we dare to point in all simplicity at the Spot we are alleged to occupy! Self-validating and self-sufficient, defying description because it offers Nothing to describe, What's seen is the Seer and his seeing, and it leaves him in no doubt about where he's coming from. Here's an experience that's uniquely immediate, intimate, and indubitable. It convinces, as nothing else can do. "There's no longer any need to believe," says the Sufi Al-Alawi, "when one *sees* the Truth."

Fourth, this experience is uniquely communicable, because it is exactly the same for all – for the Buddha, for Jesus, for Shen-hui, for Al-Alawi, for you and me. Naturally so, since there's nothing in it to differ about, nothing to go wrong, nothing idiosyncratic or merely personal and private. In headlessness we find common Ground at last. How unlike all those other experiences which are so hard to share! However vividly you describe and try to demonstrate to your companion your perceptions and thoughts and feelings, you can never be sure he is enjoying the same thing. (You and he agree to label the flower red, beautiful, interesting, and so on; but the inner experience the label is attached to is essentially a private one, impossible to get across to another. Your actual experience of red, for example, could be his experience of pink, or even blue.) But reverse the arrow of attention, and at once we enter the realm of Certainty. Here, and here alone, at the level of what's seen to be our faceless Face and true Nature, is perfect communication, everlasting agreement, no possibility of misunderstanding. This accord cannot be over-rated, because it is the profoundest at-oneness about What we and all beings *really* are. In the light of this basic assent, we can afford to differ to any degree about what we *seem* to be, about appearances.

In principle, then, this essential experience can be transmitted, without the slightest loss or distortion, to anyone who wants it. In practice, however, appropriate means of transmission are needed. Happily, they are to hand, approach 100% efficiency, and do their job in a matter of seconds. They include the pointing finger and the single eye, which we have already used here. Also the author and his friends have devised, over the last twenty years, scores of others - some of them relying on senses other than vision, many of them involving the whole body, and practically all of them suitable for work with groups of any size. (For details, consult the last three books listed at the beginning of this book, also the Postscript at the end.) Such multiplication of gates into our true Nature has much value - different gates for different temperaments, contexts, cultures, and epochs - but is neverthe-less incidental. It's convenient to have a choice of doors to our Home, but - once indoors - who cares which he came in by? Any entrance - to the place that in fact we can never leave - is a good entrance. There's no limit to them.

Fifth and last, this seeing into one's Nothingness is always on tap, whatever one's mood, whatever one is up to, however agitated or calm one happens to be at the moment - in fact, just whenever one needs it. Unlike thoughts and feelings (even the "purest" or most "spiritual" of them) it is instantly available, simply by looking in and finding no head here.

We have examined five inestimable virtues of this simple in-seeing, and found it absurdly easy, quite foolproof, deeper than deep, uniquely shareable, always to hand. But there's another side to this splendid coin, a whole set of defects or snags if you like, which experience over the last twenty years has shown up.

Some of these apparent disadvantages arise from the very advantages of this in-seeing. For instance, just because it's so obvious and easy, so available on demand and natural and ordinary, it's tragically easy to under-value, even dismiss offhand as quite trivial. In actual fact, its immense depth and spiritual power are nearly always overlooked, at least to begin with. How, it is argued, could so cheap a realization (scot-free, in fact) be worth much? Easy come, easy go. What spiritual work have we put in, by which to earn any worthwhile gift? Besides, this least expensive of realizations comes to us backed by no mystical credentials, endorsed by no burst of cosmic consciousness, no ecstasy. Quite the contrary, it's an all-time low rather than a high, a valley rather than one of those famous peak experiences. What's "Himalayan" about it, indeed? Truly it's misleading that the opening of this book should be set in those mountains, with all their lofty spiritual associations, thus obscuring the essential lowliness and ordinariness of what happened to happen there. Seeing one's true Face, in all its homely plainness, is at least as easy in a traffic jam or a public lavatory, and much less likely to be confused with any kind of attainment. And in any case the actual experience - in contrast to its setting, whether grand or dreary - cannot be treasured and got out from time to time for loving inspection, cannot be remembered at all. It is NOW, or never. It is to be found only in the Timeless Zone.* What you are neither has nor needs any time to amount to anything whatever.

No wonder, then, that seeing It (which is not other than consciously being It) is such a bare and austere and even sombre experience. The fact that it comes across as "non-religious" and "devoid of emotion", as "cold scientific evidence or matter-of-factness", as "prosaic and non-glorious", is evidence of its authenticity. "Here is nothing painted in bright colours; all is grey and extremely unobtrusive and unattractive." Such are the unenthusiastic comments which the initial seeing into Nothingness is apt to excite, and with good reason. (Our quotations are in fact from the noted Zen expert D.T. Suzuki, and he is describing satori, which is the same seeing of our true Face or Void Nature.) As for our earning this seeing, or somehow achieving What it discloses, the idea is nonsense; for it is seeing into What we and all beings eternally are, into the Timeless Zone we are all living from, regardless of merit and aside from all mystical graces – or lack of them.

The truth is that such "defects" or "snags" – in particular the seeming shallowness of this inseeing – aren't so much defects as initial misapprehensions, readily cleared up. The real "snag" is quite different, and appears extremely serious. It is that the great

*To check the whereabouts of this Zone, read off the time registered by your watch over there on your wrist, and go on reading it as you slowly bring the watch forward all the way to your eye – to the place where it registers no time, to the place where no-thing remains to undergo change and so record time, to the place where no-one remains to be born or die or wake up or fall asleep, to the place of "the true seeing, the eternal seeing". In brief, to the place where you are YOURSELF, and at Home forever.

(This may make uplifting reading, but remains no more than ideas – unless our little experiment is *actually carried out,* in a spirit that values the Obvious all the more highly when it is ridiculously obvious!)

majority of people who have been shown This, who have been induced briefly to look within and perceive their headlessness in the manner we have indicated (and their number now runs well into five figures), are happy to leave the experience at that. For them (if it's interesting at all) it's little more than an intriguing adventure, an unusual way of looking at things; or else just good fun, a pleasant sort of children's game, and in any case of no importance in day-to-day life. It's not for prolonging or repeating or studying, and certainly not for practising. And so *it has virtually no effect whatever.*

Why this near-universal refusal to take seriously what, the adepts assure us, is the best of news, carrying immense practical implications? In the case of cheerfully incurious and self-satisfied people, stuck with their unexamined beliefs and aims, the answer is obvious. What chance of unsettling all that? (And what need or right have we to attempt anything of the sort? After all, in each is hidden the One who knows just what can and what can't at this time be usefully assimilated, and who is already and forever that Enlightenment, that inner Light, all are living from.) In the case of sincere seekers, the answer is only slightly less obvious: who of us would want to become finders, as long as our search so meaningfully – so nobly! – structures our time and wards off boredom, and as long as the Nothing – which some say lies at the end of our quest – reads at this safe distance much more like an unveiled threat than a veiled promise? No, we have every reason to remain humble seekers! We are *not* enlightened! The fact is that in us all lurks an existential terror, a powerful and altogether natural resistance to what – seemingly – amounts to sudden death and annihilation. All that long-drawn-out and often agonizing effort, urged on by every kind of social pressure, to paper over the void within and to build on it a somebody right here, a face that belongs to oneself (instead of to everyone else), a distinct personality of one's very own, a stable character to match up to those around us - and now (God help us!) it's being exposed as not just a collapsing card-castle but (to the degree that it stands up at all) as the cause of our troubles! This is bad news indeed, and specially for those of us who seem to be progressing quite satisfactorily through this "vale of soul-making". The foundation of the whole personal-growth-industry is dynamited by the simple act of in-seeing. No wonder some people are visibly disturbed - embarrassed, insulted, scared, nauseated, angry, occasionally violent - when invited to look within, and shy away from the horror instantly. Nor is it a merely adult and socially induced horror: witness the case of Poppy who, at $2\frac{1}{4}$ years, was already frightened of her Emptiness.* The real wonder is that any of us - in spite of all interior resistances and exterior discouragements - should welcome and see through to the end the work of demolition. It always was a tiny minority who have this urge, and their numbers show few signs of growing rapidly. Are they naïve ones who, remaining in touch with their faceless childhood, never quite grew up; or sadly inadequate ones so hurt by life that a sort of death would seem a relief; or doubting ones for whom our language and beliefs - and specially the religious sort - are a dubious and ill-founded system of defences against what can't be doubted, namely our true Nature; or inquisitive ones so addicted to self-discovery that no price is too high to pay for it; or just unworthy recipients of divine grace? Or some combination of these types? In looking at his or her own case, the reader has quite a selection to choose from.

Anyhow (whatever the explanation) it comes about that, while this simple in-seeing is *potentially* all we have claimed for it (and much more), it is actually - for almost everybody - just

* See p. 38

49

another passing experience among the myriads that go to make up a human life. You couldn't even call it a first step along the Way; or, if you could, it's the sort of first step that *doesn't* count.

Some, however, do go on. They come to our Fifth Stage.

(5) Practising Headlessness

Now the "hard" part begins, which is the repetition of this headless seeing-into-Nothingness till the seeing becomes quite natural and nothing special at all; till, whatever one is doing, it's clear that nobody's here doing it. In other words, till one's whole life is structured round the double-barbed arrow of attention, simultaneously pointing in at the Void and out at what fills it. Such is the essential meditation of this Way. It is meditation for the market-place, in fact for every circumstance and mood, but it may usefully be supplemented by regular periods of more formal meditation – for example, a daily sitting in a quiet place enjoying exactly the same seeing, either alone or (better) with friends.

Here, in fact, is a meditation which doesn't threaten to divide our day into two incompatible parts – a time of withdrawal and quiet recollection, and a time of self-forgetful immersion in the world's turmoil. On the contrary, the whole day comes to have the same feel, a steady quality throughout. Whatever we have to do or take or suffer can thus be turned to our immediate advantage: it provides just the right opportunity to notice Who is involved. (To be precise, absolutely involved yet absolutely uninvolved.) In short, of all forms of meditation this is among the least contrived and obtrusive, and (given time to mature) the most natural and practical. And amusing too: it's as if one's featureless Original Face wore a smile like that of the disappearing Cheshire Cat!

At first, the essential practice requires much effort of attention. Normally, one takes years or decades to arrive at anything like steady and spontaneous in-seeing. Nevertheless the method is quite simple and the same throughout. It consists of ceasing to overlook the looker – or rather, the absence of the looker. Some find the practice very hard going for a very long time. Others – notably younger seers who have devoted fewer years and less effort to building the fictitious person at the centre of their universe – take to it more readily. This is to be expected: for they are still close to Stage (1) when, as infants, we were not yet objects or things for ourselves. Like animals, we then lived without complications from our central No-thingness, unconsciously. Now our intention is to get back in and live consciously from it.

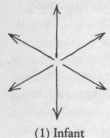

(1) Infant

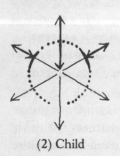

(2) Child

This intention is an inspiring one. It is nothing less than swimming with the powerful undertow of evolution – the evolution of consciousness itself through prehistory and history, and now being recapitulated in one's own history as an individual*. As the animal and infant of Stage (1), you were unselfconscious: all your arrows of attention were aimed outwards: you *overlooked your presence.* As the child of Stage (2), you probably were from time to time truly Self-conscious; on those occasions an arrow of attention was turned inwards also, and it hit the mark: *you saw your Absence*– accidentally as it were. But more and more your inward-pointing arrows fell far short of that mark: instead of getting through to the central Absence-of-any-body they got stuck in the

---

*Strictly speaking, of course, it's not consciousness itself – i.e. aware Emptiness – that evolves, but what occupies it. The timeless and absolute consciousness which you are (for which some reserve the term Awareness) must not be confused with its temporal and relative aspect, as it takes on and discards endless functions, forms, and realizations.

51

(3) Adult

(4) & (5) Seer

peripheral presence of a very human some-body. As the adult of Stage (3), and falsely self-conscious, you went on aiming your arrows of attention at that insubstantial some-body, at that human appearance of yours which daily became more substantial for you, and soon was your identity card, your identity itself. (Forged card, mistaken identity!) And now, as the seer of Stages (4) and (5), you are again truly Self-conscious: but this time you penetrate that ring of appearances more deliberately and consist-ently, and begin to rest in What they are appearances *of,* in your Reality, which is your true Identity, your Presence-Absence, your Core and Source. More and more often your arrows of attention, simultaneously aimed inwards and outwards, hit their mark. You are becoming adept at *two-way looking* – at once looking in at No-thing and out at every-thing. You are turning out to be one of those mutants in our species – seers sporadically cropping up throughout the past few thousand years – who hopefully herald the next evolutionary leap forward: who, in fact, point the way to the species' best chance of survival itself. Meantime, you are getting on with our meditation for life in the world as it is now.

At this point we have to put two important practical questions:

(i) The first is: how steady and maintained is our meditation? Is it possible – after enough practice – to be vividly Self-aware all the while, and never lose sight of the Absence right here? Ramana Maharshi, when asked about this, gave a highly significant answer. Sometimes, he explained, the Self-awareness of the *jnani* is to the forefront like the treble melody in music. At other times it lies in the background like the bass accompaniment, which you hardly notice till perhaps it stops: you were hearing it all the time, but in a subdued fashion. The heartening fact is that true Self-consciousness, when sufficiently valued and established, can be trusted to go on at some level without any fuss or concern about keeping it up deliberately. It's rather like being in love. You don't adore that person less if for hours you never recall his or her face or name: it's the commitment which remains there all along, uninterrupted, which matters. So it is with Self-realization. Once it has got hold of you it will not let you go. Your true Nature has its own way of growing more and more blatantly obvious: imperceptibly it takes over. Any attempt to force on it an artificial goal-seeking discipline can only frustrate its maturing, or even become a kind of idolatory – a pursuit of headlessness for its own sake, an attempt to make this No-thing into a much-sought-after Some-thing.

(ii) The second question is: how far can our meditation be relied upon to clear up our problems? How effective is it as psychotherapy?

The Headless Way – in contrast to those that combine Eastern spirituality with Western psychotherapy – is not concerned with deliberately watching the processes of the mind, or with psychological probing as such, or with meditation aimed at raising repressed mental material to the surface: or (for that matter) with stilling the mind. Rather it takes the line of Ramana Maharshi, who taught: "To inhere in the Self is the thing. Never mind the mind." And of Chang Chen Chi, who (in his valuable guide *The Practice of Zen*) points out that Zen isn't interested in the many aspects and strata of the mind but in penetrating to its core, "for it holds that once this core is grasped, all else will become relatively insignificant and crystal clear." Our own position is this: of course it's crucial that our psychological problems – in fact whatever thoughts and feelings happen to arise – should be clearly seen for what they are, but always *along with What they are coming from, along with Who is supposed to have them. Their Seer must not be lost sight of.* The clinical value of modern psychotherapeutic techniques isn't in question, nevertheless our radical answer to psychological problems (as to all the rest) is two-way attention – simultaneously looking in at this absolutely stainless and pollution-free and unproblematical Nothingness and out at whatever murky problems it's presenting. Their ultimate solution lies in firmly placing them off-Centre where murky things belong, not in trying to clear up the murk itself. To use the matchless Eastern image, it's a hugely reassuring fact that the purest and most exquisite of flowers – the lotus of enlightenment – blooms in the muddiest and unhealthiest of lowland swamps, amid the mire of the passions, of all that sordid and silly mind-stuff, of all our evil and pain. Clean up the swamp (what a hope!) or try to transplant the lotus amid the aseptic upland snows of an otherworldly and esoteric spirituality, and it withers. Zen goes so far as to say that the passions *are* enlightenment, the swamp *is* the lotus.

As always, our method consists in submission to the obvious, to the exoteric, before hurrying on to interpret and rectify it – a submission leading to the ever-renewed discovery that the Given is not, after all, so desperately in need of our anxious manipulation. In fact, humility in the face of the "inner" and "outer" evidence (namely, our perfect central Reality, absolutely distinct from yet absolutely one with its all-too-imperfect psycho-physical manifestations, its regional appearances, its whole setting) is what's needed for our healing. This two-way attention, cleansed of one-way intention, is sufficient to liberate us from all ill. It uncovers the Truth that sets us free – free at Home where there's no thing to accept traces or imprints, to bind us or go wrong, and where the view out, into the realm of things that seem always to be going wrong, is all right too. Yes: perfectly all right, no matter how threatening that scene appears when Home and its safety are overlooked, and we foolishly imagine we are separate persons or egos out there in the thick of it all, terrifyingly at risk. There, our delusion of egocentricity brings endless troubles down on our head; here, our realization of zerocentricity not only wards them off – head and all – but wholly transforms them. Seen from its Origin, the surrounding murk begins to take on a Beauty that's beyond beauty and ugliness, and at last our thoughts and feelings and actions are spontaneously contributing to that ultimate Beauty.

Our two-way meditation, then, is truly radical psychotherapy – psychotherapy so deep that overt and particular results may be very slow indeed to surface. Nevertheless, when sufficiently persisted in, it is sure to yield – more as a bonus than an expected reward – quite specific improvements in that "outer" scene, in the problem-ridden realm of our everyday lives. Typically, these will include an enlivening of the senses (raising the screen which muffles the plangency of sounds, dims the glow of colours, blurs forms, and filters out the loveliness shining in the "ugliest" places) and (to go with the sensory awakening) a complex of interrelated psychophysical changes – including a sustained "whole-body" alertness in place of the "heady" intermittent sort (as if one were poised through-and-through to run the race of one's life), a reduction of stress, particularly in the region of the eyes and mouth and neck (as if one were at last letting them go), a progressive lowering of one's centre of gravity (as if losing one's head were finding one's heart, and guts, and feet, which are now rooted in the Earth), a striking downward shift of one's breathing (as if it were a belly-function), and in fact a general come-down (as if all the good things one had vainly strained after in the heights were awaiting one in the depths). And, balancing this descent, a general uplift, including a sense of exaltation (as if one were perfectly straight-backed and as tall as the sky), an upsurge of creativity, rising energy and confidence, a new and childlike spontaneity and playfulness, and above all a lightness (as if one were not so much gone with the wind as the wind itself). And finally, perhaps, a calming of fears, a marked reduction of greed and anger, a smoothing out of personal relations, more capacity for selfless love, more joy. Perhaps! As a rule, however – particularly after the initial thrill and novelty of Self-realization have worn off, and the enjoyment of one's true Nature is dimmed by expectation of benefits for one's human nature – those benefits are experienced as modest, patchy and variable. The outward fruits of in-seeing aren't nearly so abundant as one would naturally wish, are slow to ripen, and even then are probably more apparent to others than to oneself. Often there is no sense of improvement whatever. There may well be growing disappointment, a sense of something more needed, additional to the bare seeing. Which brings us to the next stage of our journey.

(6) Working It Out

We have to go on to discover much more about the meaning of headlessness, its value for living, its drastic implications for our thinking, our behaviour and relationships, our role in society. This stage, even less clear-cut than the others, is bound to overlap them to a large extent, and in fact is never finished with. There's no standard pattern.

Much will depend upon the individual's gifts and temperament, and the extent to which he or she is able to link up with – and get support from – others. Certainly it's much pleasanter and easier to progress along this Way, and to make the discoveries that belong to this stage of it, in the company of friends rather than alone. All the same, neither loneliness nor any other difficulty will hold anyone back, and everything – just the right books, teachers, circumstances – will leap to his assistance, if he's determined to press on.*

It isn't only the discipline and backing provided by the group, but also the faithful and often humbling spiritual direction provided (not always intentionally) by one or another of its members, which for most of us is indispensable. Anyhow the author can testify that – whenever he lacked (or wilfully supposed he lacked) the equivalent of a roshi, guru, confessor, or spiritual director – his vision of the way ahead has been unnecessarily myopic and his track meandering.

"Alas I have no 'headless' or 'seeing' friends!" the novice seer complains. In fact, he has many: it's just that he doesn't know them. And sooner or later and given enough patience, he can have ones he does know: for this (as we've seen) is the most shareable of experiences, and the perfect instrument of communication is – literally – to hand. He should not be discouraged when people react negatively – for to throw out this insight they must first have taken it in, and moved one step nearer the time when it's allowed to stay. Nor need he be at a loss when they strike back, (for instance arguing that what they are being shown is too exclusively visual: how can it be valid – let alone important – if it isn't backed up by the other senses, and is impossible to demonstrate to a blind man?). For reasons we have already explored, the very suggestion of headlessness is for many people profoundly offensive, and there's no end to the objections they will raise. Never mind: headlessness is for living always, for sharing occasionally, for arguing about never.

Insofar as there is an "answer" to that particular objection

*The Postscript to this book makes practical suggestions about how the seer can link up with other seers.

about the blind man, it could well take the form of a small experiment. "Go blind", and "see" if you are headless, or not. Will you, the reader, kindly do just that? Shut your eyes, and for ten seconds check whether you now have the slightest evidence of a headpiece occupying the centre of your world, of a some-thing here that has any discernable boundaries or shape or size or colour or opacity – let alone eyes or nose or ears or mouth. (Aches and tickles and tastes and so on don't begin to make up a head, aren't like that at all.) Or, for that matter, have you the slightest evidence right now of a body? To make sure, how many toes can you count, when with closed eyes you drop memory and imagination and go by what's given at this moment?

In fact, the author's blind friends assure him they perceive with perfect clarity their absence of head and of body, and the presence of their true Nature as Emptiness or Space or Capacity for whatever's being experienced – including "bodily" sensations of every kind. On this journey of journeys the sighted have no real advantage over the blind. The true seeing, the eternal seeing, is everyone's.

For all of us, our two-way meditation is essentially the same, whatever sense we happen to be deploying. Always the set-up is two-sided yet absolutely asymmetrical. That bird-song drops into the Silence here; the taste of those strawberries makes itself felt against this steady background of No-taste; that horrid smell arises in contrast to this on-going absence-of-smell, to this Freshness; and so on. Similarly our thoughts and feelings appear only on the blank screen here which Zen calls No-mind, and leave no trace on it as they disappear. Just as, when I "confront" you, it's your face there presented to my absence-of-face here – face to no-face – so, whatever I'm taking in, I have to be free of: to be filled with water the cup has to be empty of it. The difference is total. This doesn't mean that, engaged in our two-way "medita-

tion for the marketplace," we think of all this: we just get on with
the job of not losing touch with our Absence.

All of which goes to show how many and varied are the roads
to Home and how the blind, like the deaf, are very well able to
travel our Way. However, the sighted are blessed with some
travel aids that are denied to the rest. (This isn't surprising; it's
not for nothing that the enlightened are called seers and not
hearers or smellers or touchers – and certainly not thinkers. Sight
is naturally the king of the senses here: when simultaneously
directed inwards and outwards, it is the arch-enemy of the
obscure, arch-revealer of the Obvious.) In the following selection
from the many realizations awaiting us (if they seem more earthy
– and sometimes more funny – than spiritual, that's much in their
favour!) it will be easy to distinguish the less important ones
which are dependent on external vision from the more important ones which are not.

(i) In appearance I'm a thing moving about in Space. In reality
I'm that unmoving Space Itself. Walking across the room, I look
down, and my head (no-head) is the infinite and empty Stillness in
which those arms and legs are flailing. Driving my car, I look *out*,
and my human body (no-body) is this same Stillness, in which the
whole countryside is being shuffled like a giant's pack of cards.
Going out at night, I look *up*, and my Earth body (no-Earth-body)
is the same Stillness in which those heavenly bodies are swinging
and dancing. (No: I can find no head here to turn to and fro, to
bob up and down!) Finally and most importantly, I "go blind"
(shut my eyes, they say) and my Universe body (no-Universe-
body) is the same infinite and empty Stillness, now revealing
itself as the unmoving No-mind whose mental contents refuse to
stay still for a moment. Besides confirming yet again one's true
Identity, this aspect of our submission to the Obvious – of our
two-way looking, our meditation for all seasons – happens to take

the rush out of "the rush of modern life": or rather, out of the one who thinks he rushes. He never moved an inch. All his agitation is illusory. He neither needs nor can do anything to calm down – except stop overlooking the place where he is forever at rest, where the Peace that passes all understanding is so brilliantly self-evident. This yearned-for tranquillity, which he imagined was always evading him, is discovered at his very centre, *begging to be noticed!*

(ii) While I appear to others over there (viewing me from a distance) to be a mobile and limited human thing, I am really here (viewing myself from no distance) this immobile and unlimited and non-human No-thing. This No-thing or Space I perceive to be packed with all manner of things – moving, coloured, shaped, noisy, pleasant and unpleasant, sensory and non-sensory, and so on. And paradoxically, just because this Space is absolutely unlike and absolutely uncontaminated by its contents, it is absolutely identified with them. I don't believe this, I see it. The Space *is* the things that occupy it. This Stillness – Silence *is* the motions and the sounds of which it is the background. *As something I am merely that thing, as no-thing I am all things.*

(iii) And they are all given right here. Thus that sky, Sun, cloud, tree, grass, window, carpet, word-covered page, the hands holding it – all are present, obviously presented to me where I am and my camera is, and not where we are not. No distance comes between us. (As pointed out earlier, if I go up to them I progressively lose them; moreover a line stretched between us, connecting this spot with the "furthest" object, I must read as a dimensionless point.) It follows that all the world is mine, and I am rich beyond compare. And, for good measure, this kind of ownership is the only real kind. For as this tiny and solid (and quite fictional) *something* here I shut out all other things from the volume I occupy and so am the poorest of the poor; while as this immense and vacant (and real) No-thing or Space I let them in, I take delivery of the Universe, I have and hold the lot. No wonder it's all so compelling, so immediate, so - *bright!*

(iv) How is it, then, that I still go on seeing everything - beginning with these hands and ending with that blue sky - as out there instead of here? Or, strangely, as both at once? At one level, the answer is that this three-dimensional world is such a convenient way of accounting for the data, a model to whose survival-value my eyes themselves - whose physiology is so largely geared to depth-finding - bear witness. At a profounder level, the answer is that, in actual fact, *it's not my world but its Viewer that is 3-D.* Here in me - on *my* side of this inward-pointing finger, of this page, of every object - there stretches this unplumbed Chasm. (To it I owe the happy - if paradoxical - fact that the star-sprinkled sky, though no longer distant from me by an angstrom, is nevertheless more other, more awesomely celestial - than ever it was: lending it unlimited distance from my unlimited resources, I lend it unlimited enchantment.) One way or another, the flatland of my infancy had to go. Throughout childhood and early adulthood, *my method was to push the world away, to award it distance of its own.* Result: I lost it, of course. Increasingly my projection of it amounted to my rejection of it and rejection by it, and I grew more and more impoverished, lonely, cut off, alienated. The initial survival-value of that method was rapidly going into reverse and becoming (so to say) extinction-value. But now at last, as the seer of later stages, instead of pushing it all away I let it all in again, and the world is fathomless because I am fathomless. The double-barbed arrow of my attention is simultaneously pointing ahead to the "outer" world of things which in fact start and stop right here, and back to the "inner" world of the No-thing which in fact goes on and on for ever. And they are one world. All is in me, all is mine, all is me, and I am well again.

(v) What I truly own works for me, not against me. If the Universe is mine, it should behave the way I want it to. Well, the truth is that, mirror-like, this Capacity or Emptiness which I am has no way of refusing any of its contents, no preferences or favourites. It must surrender to whatever occurs. It is choiceless, and yet (as will become increasingly clear as we go on) it is responsible for everything that comes about. It wills nothing, and all things.

(vi) Even my own actions become acceptable. My silliest mistakes are somehow not mistakes after all. And anyway, whatever I'm doing – from washing the dishes to driving my car to thinking about this paragraph – I find myself doing it worse while I'm imagining a headed somebody right here doing it, and better while I'm seeing him off. Consciously living from the truth of the No-thing-I-am works much, much better than living from the lie of the thing-I'm-not – which is hardly surprising.

(vii) It's all a matter of putting first things first, of never losing touch with THIS. When as a person I aim *directly* to be out in front and involved in life and truly *with* it, I am in fact alienated from life, up against it, ultimately its victim. Whereas when my aim is *indirect* – via the perceived Absence here of that person seeking involvement – why then I'm not just out in the world, not just *with* it: I'm relishing the experience of *being* it. I'm at large, world-asserting, *enlightened* (as Zen master Dogen so delightfully puts it) *by all beings*. Enlightened by what they seem to be, as well as What they are.

(viii) I come to realize that my seeing into the Absence here isn't seeing into *my* Absence, but everyone's. I see that the Void here is void enough and big enough for all, that it is *the* Void. Intrinsically, we all are one and the same, and there are no others. It follows that what I do to anyone I do to myself, and what happens to them happens to me. It's a fact that I must take very seriously. Call it unconditional love, or compassion, or a truly generous heart – without this, and the spontaneous living out of this, my in-seeing is tentative indeed.

(ix) Seeing into No-thingness is consciously connecting up with the Source of all thingness, with the originality of the Origin and the creativity of the Creator, with the fountainhead of all truly spontaneous feeling and action and what is new and therefore unpredictable. As always, this isn't for believing but for testing. See, and see what you get up to!

(x) This seeing is coming Home to the only safe harbour, to our dear native land (profoundly familiar yet inexhaustably mysterious), to what's trustworthy. This again is for checking, all day and every day.

These ten, with countless other realizations, await the traveller at this stage of the journey. They lead to – they are evidence of – the deepening and maturing of his or her original headlessness. Or (better put) they are part of the working out of what all along was implicit in that vision.

Prominent among them all is a realization – a many-sided spiritual development appropriate to our Stage (6) but certainly not confined to it – which insists on special attention at this point. It is the experience of *unknowing*, of one's profound and all-inclusive ignorance. In fact, it follows from "I am nothing" that "I know nothing", for obviously an *informed* nothing is not a nothing but a something, form and not void.

This unknowing falls into two quite distinct parts:

(1) The first is the abandonment of our assumption that *of course* things are and have to be what they are. It is giving up our adult, sophisticated, man-or-woman-of-the-world assurance that (as we say) we know it all, that we've seen it all before, that there's nothing new under the Sun, that we have it all taped, that "wow!" is childish and a yawning "so what?" is grown-up. (Sud-

63

denly raise your little finger, blink an eyelid, notice the hospitality you're according to these printed shapes and those sounds – the vividness they owe to the depth and clarity of the room you give them – and admit you have no idea *how* you perform these and a million other miracles.) It is a kind of global forgetting, a laundering of our soiled universe, washing away accumulated layers of names, memories, associations, and leaving it all unfamiliar and fresh and sweet-smelling. It is ceasing to take everything and anything for granted. It is the re-discovery of the obvious as very strange, the given as wonderful and precious, before we bend it to our purposes. It is admitting the glory that was there all along. It is actually *looking* at the "meanest" stone and fallen leaf, at the "nastiest" piece of garbage, at "irrelevant" things like the shape and colour of shadows and the reflection of coloured city lights in wet roads at night (which we've ceased to see because we don't drive round them). It is consciously being what we really are – Capacity for things – the Space in which each of them is allowed to arrive at its peculiar kind of perfection. It is consciously viewing everything from its Source, reuniting it with the Infinity that lies *this* side of it. It is seeing, hearing, smelling, touching things as if for the first time, relieved of the crushing load of time past. It is the revitalizing and extension of our childhood astonishment. It is being present at creation's morning, before Adam named the creatures and got bored with them. It is seeing them with their Creator's eye, as very good. In Zen terms, again, it is "being enlightened by all beings," because there's nothing here to cloud their light.

This unknowing has no limits. It extends beyond what we perceive to all we feel and think and do. It is ceasing to know how to cope with life, where we are going, what to do after this immediate task is done, what's going to happen to us tomorrow, next week, next year. It is walking one step at a time and blindfold, in the assurance that the Space here – which is nothing and knows nothing but Itself – will nevertheless come up, moment by moment, with what's needed. It is living like the lilies of the field, taking no thought for the morrow, trusting our Source. (Of course, this can be used as an excuse for dropping out, but when *lived* it is dropping in and giving to life all we're capable of, including whatever planning is necessary.)

The life of unknowing, and the extraordinary joy and workability of it, are not to be aimed at directly. They can only be had by giving up any claim to them and any idea of their cultivation. However, they may be counted on to arrive in their own good time, provided we attend to their background, to the Nothingness here. Seek first this barest of Kingdoms (the Kingdom within) and all these beautiful things will be added: seek them, and they will be taken away. Let us stay with the Emptiness we know (and unknow) so well, and It will supply the filling that we don't know at all, but which will turn out to be exactly what's required at this moment.

Why should we trust It always to come up with the right answer, however wrong that answer may currently seem? Why should we trust It *absolutely?* If our experience hasn't yet given us overwhelming reason for doing so, let's now look at what is Its sublimest, most brilliant, confidence-inspiring and mind-boggling (yet, once seen, most obvious) accomplishment of all.

(2) The second category of unknowing isn't the giving up of our assumption that of course things have to be what they are, or what we make of them, but that they *have to be at all!* Why should existence itself exist? The difference between these two unknowings is immeasurable; they aren't in the same class. The first sees as miracles the things we are aware of. The second sees as *the* Miracle the aware No-thing from which they come. The first is comparatively mild, gently on-going, ever-changing, a matter of

degree. The second is a knock-out, an all-or-nothing insight not remotely like any other.

However, the key to it is miniscule, and it lies in the distance between those little words, *what* and *that*. Here, *WHAT reality is* loses all importance, *THAT reality is* becomes all-important. Ludwig Wittgenstein wrote; "*What* things are in the world is a matter of complete indifference to what is higher. God does not reveal himself *in* the world ... It is not *what* things are in the world that is mystical, but *that* it exists." Which I would expand to: the truly mystical fact is that *God* – alias Self-aware Being – exists, and after him the existence of his world is comparatively unremarkable, a matter of course.

At this point I shall have to revert to straight autobiography. I cannot, of course, remember in detail the early episodes in my much interrupted (but lifelong and passionate) love-affair with the Mystery of Existence. Nevertheless the following reconstruction of that four-stage adventure – culminating in the discovery of the ultimate meaning and value of "having no head" – is the best way of conveying the spirit of it, the actual feel of it:

(i) I am a young teenager, in conversation with an older friend:

DH: All right, God made the world, but how did he come to be there in the first place? *Who made God?*

Friend: No-one. He created himself.

DH: But how could he do that? Was there nothing at all, a great big blank, and then – BANG! – there he was? He must have been *flabbergasted!* I can hear him shouting: "Look, I've just made myself happen! Aren't I *clever!*"

Friend: You're being irreverent. God is so great that he always was, he always *had* to be. Why should he be flabbergasted at his own existence? It's his nature.

DH: Well, *I* think he must get goose pimples every time he notices what he's done – producing himself like that out of thin air (not just as a sleepy old lump of something but wide-awake), with no outside help at all! It's not just magic, it's *impossible!* After that, he can do anything: make billions of worlds all complete, with his hands tied behind his back!

Friend: You don't understand. There *has* to be Someone, creating everything.

DH: But not Someone creating himself! *He* didn't have to happen. He might not have got round to it. Or, if he *did* have to happen, there must have been Someone else in the background, making him happen - which means he isn't God after all. The real God is that Someone else - again, busy inventing himself!

Friend: (getting up to go): These things aren't our business. God and the beginning are mysteries we aren't meant to probe - mysteries to us of course, but not to him.

DH: (to himself): Then why ever did he make me a prober? I still think it's very funny - funny-peculiar - that there's anyone and anything at all. There ought to be just - nothing! Not a speck, not a twinge, not a glimmer of awareness.

(ii) The time is some years later. Now grown up - but not yet consciously headless - I reflect further on the subject of Self-existence, which will not let me alone.

It is God himself who is the arch-unknower! God (or whatever you call him or her who is No-thingness and Source and Awareness and Being) can't possibly understand how he gave rise to himself, how he pulled himself up by his own bootstraps out of blank non-existence, how he woke himself from that deepest of sleeps, from that long and dreamless night. To understand himself would be to stand under himself in an infinite and futile regression. An absurd and self-defeating contortion! He *loves* being an absolute mystery to himself - a God who had himself eternally taped would suffer eternal boredom. Nor is this divine ignorance a shortcoming in his nature. Quite the reverse: it's the reason why he stands forever in rapturous awe of himself, beyond all measure. It's the reason for his much-more-than-human humility, his trembling in the face of his own unspeakable grandeur, his vertigo as he gazes into his own bottomless depths. (Only we complacent humans are conceited enough to claim Being as our natural right, as much in the bag, and to be taken for granted, as if we had it served up regularly for breakfast!) And, when at last our ridiculous pretension wears thin, it's the ultimate reason, not only for our adoration of him, but also for unlimited trust and optimism. After this initial and only real Miracle, what miracle can be ruled out? All things are possible for the One who has achieved the Impossible. The One who has the great know-how - which is knowing and not knowing how to be - is no bungler. His world has not gone wrong. All is well.

(iii) I have now come to my early thirties, and have "lost my head". As a result, my childhood and youthful wonder at Existence begins to take on new dimensions. I stumble with delight on that luminous and inspired saying of St. John of the Cross: "They who know God most perfectly perceive most clearly that he is perfectly incomprehensible." And this leads to the startling thought: what validates our knowledge of him (as perfectly incomprehensible), what makes it true knowledge, is that it is really his knowledge of himself, going on in us. For it isn't as these little, opaque, headed, all-too-human creatures that we are stunned, bowled over, by the wonder of Self-creation, but as the Self-Creator himself. (No: we aren't indulging in delusions of grandeur! On the contrary, we are dismissing as ludicrous all our claims to *personal* divinity. The real arrogance, the real blasphemy is the pretence that this human being *as such* can climb to the giddy heights from which God can be viewed at all - to say nothing of the underlying pretence that this human "being" at its own level has any being of its own apart from the One who *is*.) The stupendous fact (at once infinitely exalting and infinitely humbling) is that our amazed delight in his achievement is nothing less than his own amazed delight - the real thing and no reflection of it, or even participation in it. At this level, what others are there for him to share it with?

(iv) Finally, all of a sudden the crowning (and at last perfectly obvious) truth dawns on me. Self-origination isn't an impossible feat pulled off by someone else, far away, once and for all, long ago, but is going on right here and right now! The Impossibility is sustained, inexhaustible and ever present. Here, in this despised, they tell me tiny, overlooked place, supposedly bunged up with a head, *here the whole wildly extravagant drama of Self-creation is being enacted as if for the first time* (omit *as if!*) *in all its pristine wonder, at this very instant!* Right here and now, this mind-blowing mystery - this shout "I AM!" - is *my* shout, is - *my* mystery, is *my* Self. I have to take it on board. Right here and now, I can no longer evade my responsibility for Isness itself - let alone for all that is.

If at the very centre of my universe there had been a blob - a little and tightly packed and intensely personal box-full of neural material and processes - how crazy to suppose that such a puny thing could meaningfully encompass the Cosmos and its origin and the whole mystery of Being! Fortunately I perceive - I could say this headless Place itself perceives - that as absolutely uncluttered and infinitely extended Awareness it is ideally fitted for that tremendous task. That's its proper business. What's more, I can be sure that this same meanest yet grandest, most private yet least private, nearest and best known yet least known of places, packs many more - immeasurably more - surprises, unimaginably marvellous. Who would have thought that losing a mere head would mean gaining such a treasure house?

However, the very richness of this potentiality, the unlimited resources of this Aladdin's Cave, can become a reason for frustration, for the anxious feeling that, after all, we are forever condemned to remain seekers – never able to get it all, always missing something important, always on the brink of *the* revelation. But this anxiety only comes up insofar as we lose sight of the Cave Itself, of *What* is so prolific, of the Transparent Source and Container and indeed the Ending of all realizations, our true and eternal and natureless Nature. They are born; It is unborn. They come and go, wax and wane; It never changes. They are built of thoughts and feelings; It is clear of them. Not even the sublimest of these realizations, not even the crowning wonder of Self-origination,* is Real in the sense that *It* is Real, and none is for grasping at or hanging onto. Yet each is to be taken, as it emerges, with reverence, as carrying the authority of its Origin and perfectly suited to its time and occasion.

In fact, we have by no means come to the end of those great realizations which mark out the stages of the Headless Way. We still have far to go along that track. Moreover the going is about to get harder and harder. A formidable Barrier is looming up...

(7) The Barrier

No matter how revolutionary the discoveries made along Stages (5) and (6) of the Way, or how valuable for living they are beginning to prove, in the end they leave the wayfarer profoundly unsatisfied. There remains an ache, an undefined longing. In spite of all this quite genuine spiritual "progress", an all-import-

---

* *The Gospel of the Egyptians* invokes the "self-begotten Perfect One, who art not outside me," and the *Tripartite Tractate* speaks of the ineffable One who "knows himself as he is, namely as the one who is worthy of his own admiration, and glory, and honour, and praise, *since he produces himself.*" The Gnostic authors of these passages lived around the 2nd – 3rd century A.D. In 1657 the Catholic Angelus Silesius pictures God as "bending and bowing to himself." He is wondrous because "he wills that which he is and is that which he wills, with no end and no cause."

ant region remains untravelled, or at least insufficiently explored. It's a dark and dangerous country inhabited by monsters, and it cannot be by-passed. It is the area of the will. Here, beyond and beneath all these luminous goings-on, the unregenerate ego is still at work, possibly beavering away more vigorously than ever. And so we come to Stage (7) of our Way, which looks much more like a dead end or impassable obstruction than what it is in fact – the really testing stage of the journey, painful but obligatory.

It's a disappointing and perhaps quite devastating discovery, that one's perfectly clear and near-habitual seeing into the Nothing here (backed by all those encouraging developments we noticed earlier) can go along with blindness to a massive Something here – namely, one's personal and separative will or ego. It's as if one's eye (perception) and head (thinking) had been opened and flooded with light, while one's heart and entrails remained at least partially closed and dark. As if one were *half* surrendered – the upper part completely, while the lower may be protesting like mad. To some degree the "higher" and more conscious regions of the total personality have become at variance with – and split off from – the "inferior" and less conscious levels. (One's case may well be worse, in this respect, than that of the "unenlightened" person who at *all* levels is committed to his fictitious thinghood, so avoiding a serious interior dichotomy.) Result: increasing and unaccounted-for stress, perhaps severe depression, a feeling of one's worthlessness and futility. A dreadful thought haunts one: was all that spiritual "progress", all that effort leading up to this Barrier, a waste of time, even fraudulent?

We can react in various ways. Deeply discouraged, we can turn back, with the sad feeling that this Way of plain seeing isn't so straightforward after all and far rougher than it promised to be: and so we leave our difficult desert track and try other, better paved and more popular and more scenic highways, booking up, perhaps, on one or other of the many guided spiritual tours that are on offer. This reaction is as common as it is understandable.

A less common response is to call a halt at this point and put to use, indeed cultivate, the special powers or *siddhis* that have already come with in-seeing or headlessness, applying them to limited (though not always narrowly personal) ends - ends which, however reasonable or even noble, are in fact set up by the separative ego. (Actually there's no ego-trip to match the spiritual ego-trip! Satan is said to be the most enlightened of all angels: the only spiritual excellence he lacks is humility, self-abandonment. Doubtless no more than a deeply significant myth; nevertheless the ego in us all is devilish enough and capable of endless twists and turns.) For example there flourish today, as in the past, various sorts of gifted spiritual adepts and miracle-workers and magicians, leaders of large-scale cults, who seek (sometimes with spectacular if temporary success) to exploit their contact with What they are, in order to promote what they are *not* - namely their false selfhood, their limited ends, their power over others, in short their ego.* At its worst this is the road to spiritual suicide. At its best, a tempting side-track which diverts for a time more than a few travellers.

The true route lies straight into and eventually through the Barrier, which our Western tradition calls the Dark Night of the Soul. Of it, Evelyn Underhill (an expert) writes: "The self in its

---

*The mark of this sort of leader is that, instead of insisting that his followers look to their own inmost Resource, and accordingly take responsibility for their lives, he encourages them to look to and rely on him. He may explain that handing over to him, the external guru, is a first step towards handing over to the internal Guru, their true Self; but in practice this second step — which requires a right-about-turn — may well get increasingly hard to take as the months and years of mounting devotion go by. On the other hand, if the guru *really* wants his disciples to break free of him as soon as possible, and turn inwards to their own Self-sufficiency, he has ways of helping them to do so — with the result that their love and gratitude can only deepen.

first purgation has cleansed the mirror of perception; hence, in its illumined life, has *seen* Reality... Now, it has got to *be* Reality: a very different thing. For this a new and more drastic purgation is needed – not of the organs of perception, but of the very shrine of the self: that 'heart' which is the seat of personality, the source of its love and will." In a certain sense, this is the real start of the Way, of the true spiritual life, which is nothing else than self-surrender, self-abandonment, actually underwriting whatever happens to one, dying as the separate and illusory ego (I am a somebody) and being reborn as the one and truly egoless Ego (I AM). It could be said that all spiritual "progress" up to this point was merely preparation for this, the essential and by far the hardest stage of the Way, leading eventually to the Breakthrough.

(8) The Breakthrough

This amounts to a profound declaration of intent. *It is the realization at gut level (so to say) that one's deepest desire is that all shall be as it is – seeing that it all flows from one's true Nature, the Aware Space here.*

How is this breakthrough actually made? What can one do to bring it nearer?

In a sense, nothing. It's not a doing but an *un*doing, a giving up, an abandonment of the false belief that there's anyone here to abandon. What else is there to do? After all, one's initial in-seeing – no matter how "brief" and "shallow" – was already total self-surrender: everything here went: or rather, it was clear there's nothing here to go. *It was the essential quantum leap from the fiction of egocentricity to the fact of zerocentricity.* And for sure the faithful day-to-day seeing put in since then – the seeing that already one *is* Nothing and Everything – is a most valuable preparation for the discovery that at the deepest level one already *wills* Nothing and Everything. Then life itself – if only we will learn its infallibly wise but often agonizing lesson – is always demonstrating that the gaining of our separate and personal goals yields only the briefest satisfaction, and after that disillusion and boredom, if not disgust: whereas, whenever we have the grace to say YES! to our circumstances, and actively to will (rather than passively to acquiesce in) whatever happens, why then there springs up that real and lasting joy which Eastern tradition calls *ananda*.

Is this breakthrough, then, an advance beyond the Obvious to what's unobvious, beyond the Ordinary to the extraordinary, beyond the secular and self-evident to esoteric, mystical, deeply hidden spiritual matters? Have we finished with the compass – namely, childlike trust in the Given – which has guided us thus far on our long journey? Quite the contrary. This side of the barrier lies the very homeland of the Ordinary, the kingdom of the Obvious, of What's So. On the other side, before the breakthrough, how severely our desires darkened and distorted and hid what there was to see, and our attachments – our love and our hate – were allowed to invade and befog our central Clarity and blind us to the real! How frequently we saw only what we wanted to see, and our intention played havoc with our attention! (Two examples of wishful hallucination: so desperately did I need to match up to those complete humans around me, that for decades I "saw" a head on *this* trunk also; and, for much the same reason, 17th century microscopists "saw" and drew human sperms as minute and elongated human beings!) *That side of the barrier our wilfulness erodes the Obvious: this side, the Obvious erodes our wilfulness.* The barrier is none other than the culminating defence-effort of our wilfulness or ego, its most formidable but desperate stand against sustained attack by the inescapable facts; and what overcomes it is more and more of the same realism, the same thankful reverence for What's So – for the Plainly Given, the Blatantly Obvious – that brought us all the way up to the barrier. In terms of our Western tradition, our breakthough is our unconditional and ever-renewed surrender to God's will as perfectly revealed in our circumstances – to God's will clearly on show all around us and within us, in the shape of all that's going on right now. *Insofar as his will becomes ours, we see his world as it is; and, insofar as we see it as it is, our will becomes his and from our hearts we welcome all that world is bringing to us.* Here, in short, our seeing and our willing merge – not once-and-for-all of course, but moment by moment, so long as life lasts.

For further light on this coming together of what we see and what we will, let's revert to our earlier quotation from one of the Buddha's sermons: "Nirvana is visible in this life, inviting, attractive, accessible to the wise disciple." What exactly is this so-visible Nirvana? In the same sermon it is described as "the Peace, the Highest... the end of craving, the turning away from desire." Here at last the split is mended; there is no wound dividing the Nothing that is so clearly *seen* from the Nothing that is now deeply *felt* – as unconditional surrender of the will. Or, to repeat the Buddha's phrase, as the end of craving.

If we may talk at all of peak experiences, this (as the Buddha assures us) is the highest of them, and it's inseparable from the lowest of valley experiences. Depth is height, read the other way round; infinite abasement is infinite exaltation; total self-loss is total self-fulfilment. This is how to get your way, at last, by stopping all pretence and being *yourself.* That great Christian authority on surrender – Jean-Pierre de Caussade – writes: "If you abandon all restraint, carry your wishes to their furthest limits, open your heart boundlessly, there is not a single moment when you will not find all you could possibly desire. The present moment holds infinite riches beyond your wildest dreams."

By way of balance – and complete contrast in style but identity in substance – here is a Zen story. A certain master had a gifted pupil, whom he decided to send to a great teacher who would put

75

the final touch to his training and point the way to the crowning Zen experience. To the pupil's astonishment, this best of teachers turned out to be a poor and rather sick old woman, from whom he could extract no teaching. However, she did in the end reveal all. It was this: "I've no complaints!"

This masterpiece of sobriety – like de Caussade's enthusiastic outpouring – is about the benediction, the ultimate joy that was all along implicit in our seeing quite simply (with a wise and blessed naïvety) that here we have no head, no thing at all. What a long way we travel to find the treasure of treasures we carry with us all the time!

Summary and Conclusion

This Way puts headlessness – alias seeing into Nothingness – at the very start of the spiritual life. From the beginning it is "the true seeing, the eternal seeing," and isn't superseded or improved or changed at all as we travel along. It's the searching but kindly Light that illumines all stages of the Way. It's the wish-fulfilling Gem, the Given – at once despised and feared – which in the end is found to give us, lovingly, all we want. Or again, it's the Rock, the Foundation supporting the multistoried fabric of religion, a fabric always under construction and always becoming dangerously lopsided – all heart or all head, ascetic or sensual, otherworldly or up-to-the-eyes in politics, etc. – and till we take our stand on that Bedrock we are somewhat off-balance, we wobble, we oscillate between extremes. Yet again (for the metaphors of This are inexhaustible) it is the very Bread of Life which, though tasteless, is the *real* nutrient, and moreover provides support for the delicacies – the spiritual and mystical delights – that are sometimes spread on it. Happily our larder, though often lacking these more appetizing supplements to our diet, never runs short of the Staff of Life.

Bringing the story up to date

Having said which, we must hasten to repeat that, by itself and when not followed up by sustained practice and deep under-standing, plus (above and below all) by surrender of the separa-tive personal will, our initial experience of headlessness is as yet unavailing. What we can say of this fugitive revelation is that (though capable of misuse) it never of itself did anybody any harm, that it does open a brief window on Eternity, and that (the hinge now loosened) the window is liable at any moment to swing wide open again in God's wind and eventually to stay wide open. What we are can be trusted to reveal Itself in all its noonday freshness and warmth and brilliance, its blazing obviousness, exactly when It should.

Postscript

Let's assume that you would like to continue along this Way. In that case, you may be asking such questions as: Where do I go from here? To whom do I look for further guidance and encouragement? What supporting group could I join?

For a spiritual movement that's as alive and as distinctive as most others, the Headless Way is remarkably lacking in organization. It resembles the people who take it up in that it, too, is without a head - in the sense that it has no presiding authority, no governing council or headquarters, and no staff looking after a duly card-indexed and paid-up membership who meet regularly and try to follow certain guidelines.

The reason for this absence of structure doesn't lie in any lukewarmness, or reluctance to disseminate the experience this book is about. Rather the reverse. It arises from the nature of that experience itself - as the ultimate in Self-reliance. Or, in more detail, from the fourfold realization that the way really to live is to look in and see Who is doing so, that only you are in a position to see this "Who", that this in-seeing establishes You as the authority on what matters supremely, and that accordingly your path will not conform to some set pattern laid down from above, by this or any other book or person or system. For example, though none of the eight stages described here can be bypassed, you may well find yourself negotiating the later ones in a different order, and certainly in a manner that's very much your own.

Looked at from outside, as a grouping of self-styled headless characters doing their thing, their apparent anarchy is at once a huge disadvantage (inasmuch as organization is necessary to get things off the ground) and something of an advantage (inasmuch as organizations spawn problems that obscure – if not undermine – those very things they were formed to advance). Looked at from inside, however, this worldly wisdom ceases to apply: our concern here isn't with things but with the No-thing they come from, with the Indefinable that reduces to nonsense all plans to put it on the map and make something of it. Why set up a Group or Faction – which at once splits humanity into us enlightened insiders and those endarkened outsiders – a Faction (if you please!) whose stated aim is to show there's *no* such split, that intrinsically they *are* us, and that we are all perfectly enlightened *already?* The truth is that the Headless Way isn't a way after all, a means of getting somewhere. Everything one's heart could possibly desire is freely given from the very start. This makes it strikingly different from those disciplines and courses which come in progressive instalments, with the real goods to be delivered some day: and meanwhile there has to be this Institution to lay down the rules and administer the whole business. Who, anyway, would join a set-up and pay good money to be given – when sufficiently trained – what he sees he already has, in full measure, pressed down and shaken together and running over?

Our overriding purpose, then – which is seeing into and living from Nothingness – is necessarily organization-resistant. For all other purposes we remain free to join whatever organizations we please. This means that, having no "church" of our own, we offer minimal challenge to others, and hopefully remain more able to learn from them and contribute to them. And in fact a number of our "headless" friends find it helpful to belong to some established religious or quasi-religious community. But the headless one remains the Only One, and sees itself as the Alone, and faces its Solitariness. At this level there are no others.

All the same – and descending now to the level where others do exist – the difficulty of keeping up this seeing by oneself, of going it alone, can scarcely be exaggerated. For the majority of us caught up in this most daring and exacting of adventures, the company of fellow-adventurers is indispensable. Accordingly it would be unrealistic – worse: irresponsible and uncaring – if we were to encourage people to take the message of this book to heart, yet fail to follow it up with all the continued support that the nature of the enterprise allows. And, in fact, we do have much to offer readers who are committed to going on:

First and foremost, there are loving friends, a network – loose, scattered, altogether informal – of seers who use every available means of keeping in touch. Second, some assistance in that aim is offered by an occasional magazine entitled SHARE IT, whose purpose includes linking headlessness with the great spiritual traditions, and indeed with all aspects of life itself. The editor is Anne Seward, Church Lane, Playford, Ipswich, England: telephone Ipswich (0473) 624556. (Here is a welcome opportunity to record that, among the many friends who helped shape the final chapter of this book, it was Anne Seward who contributed so much that she is practically its co-author.) Third, besides the large and precious (and increasingly available) mystical literature of the world – mystical in the sense that it points to our true Identity – there is a small number of books and other aids by the author: details can be found at the beginning of this book. Particulars of forthcoming workshops conducted by him and others, and designed to share headlessness, may be had from Anne Seward, to whom proposals and requests for workshops should please be sent. Fourth and last, if headless friends still prove hard to find, they may not be so hard to make. The condition, in spite of all resistances, is infectious and uniquely communicable. Anyhow, one of the best ways to keep it up is to pass it on.

But in the end all such considerations and contrivances are quite marginal. For it's not as humans – as so many separate individuals helping one another to see Who they really are – that we come to that vision, but (in the Upanishadic phrase) as "the One Seer in all beings." Self-seeing is indeed the prerogative and speciality of the One, and in the last resort all our efforts – organized or chaotic – to help that seeing along are quite hilarious.

To repeat our initial question, then: where do we go now? The answer is: nowhere. Let us resolutely stay right here, seeing and being This which is Obviousness itself, and take the consequences. They will be all right.

ARKANA – NEW-AGE BOOKS FOR MIND, BODY AND SPIRIT

A selection of titles

With over 200 titles currently in print, Arkana is the leading name in quality new-age books for mind, body and spirit. Arkana encompasses the spirituality of both East and West, ancient and new, in fiction and non-fiction. A vast range of interests is covered, including Psychology and Transformation, Health, Science and Mysticism, Women's Spirituality and Astrology.

If you would like a catalogue of Arkana books, please write to:

Arkana Marketing Department
Penguin Books Ltd
27 Wright's Lane
London W8 5TZ